Ridgeway

National Trail Companion

7th edition published February 2012

ISBN 978-0-9561074-3-5

Edited by Jos Joslin & Elaine Townson

Photos on pages: 6, 7, 13, 29, 46, 49, 51, 56, 62 (top), 66, 71, 89, 94
© *Tina Stallard/Natural England*

Photos on pages: 11, 18, 23, 35, 53, 61, 62 (bottom), 69, 73, 79, 84, 86, 93

© *Jos Joslin*

Photos on pages: 74 (top), 90 © *Chilterns Conservation Board*

Photos on pages: 34, 41 © *Mark Philpott*

Photos on pages: 74 (bottom) © *Matt Ball*

Published by

National Trails Office

Countryside Service

Signal Court

Old Station Way

Eynsham

OX29 4TL

tel 01865 810224

email Ridgeway@oxfordshire.gov.uk

website www.nationaltrail.co.uk/ridgeway

Designed by Linda Francis

tel 01865 407626

Cover photo:

Folly Clump, west of Letcombe Regis

© *Jos Joslin*

Contents

Introduction

87 miles (139km) long, much of it following the ancient chalk ridge route used by prehistoric man and surrounded by numerous historic monuments, The Ridgeway offers the chance to get away from the bustle of life in this busy part of England. Perfect, but not too strenuous, for long distance use, this Trail is also ideal for day trips or less. The whole of The Ridgeway can be enjoyed by walkers with horseriders and cyclists able to use all of the western half as far as the River Thames at Streatley and short sections further east.

The Ridgeway

INTRODUCTION 1

This guide gives you all the information you need to plan an enjoyable visit to The Ridgeway. It has details about accommodation, refreshments, shops, transport, toilets and many other facilities along this National Trail.

The Companion is not a route guide: for detailed information about the Trail itself, The Ridgeway National Trail Guide by Anthony Burton (Aurum Press, 2011) is available from most book shops or online. Alternatively it can be mail ordered from the National Trails Office (see page 16 for details). The Companion complements the Trail Guide and, armed with a copy of each, it is hoped that anyone using The Ridgeway needn't require anything more. Enjoy your trip.

One of only 15 National Trails in England and Wales, The Ridgeway starts in the famous World Heritage Site of Avebury in Wiltshire. It travels for 87 miles (139km) steadily north east along the surprisingly remote scarp ridge of the downs, across the River Thames, and through the Chiltern Hills to finish in the Iron Age fort on top of Ivinghoe Beacon in Buckinghamshire.

The western half of The Ridgeway, as far as Streatley, can be enjoyed by walkers, horseriders and cyclists, whereas only walkers can use the full extent of the eastern half. Despite its relative remoteness, public transport to The Ridgeway is pretty good, especially to the eastern half, where there are several railway stations close to the Trail and an excellent bus network. With a little planning many places along the western half can also be reached by bus or train or a combination of the two.

The Ridgeway passes through two distinctive protected landscapes, both designated Areas of Outstanding Natural Beauty (AONB). The western half of the Trail travels through the open expansive downland of the North Wessex Downs AONB, whilst east of the Thames it stays amongst the more gentle and wooded countryside of the Chilterns AONB.

In the west The Ridgeway travels as a broad ancient track along the open and fairly isolated top of the chalk downland ridge, often several kilometres from the nearest village. Here, to the south is rolling downland and to the north, at the bottom of the steep scarp slope, the wide expanse of the Thames Valley. The far-reaching views are

dominated by the sky, the clouds and small clumps of beech woodland and all you may have for company is a solitary skylark singing overhead or a hare chasing across an adjacent field.

In the past these downs were sheep grazed, but since the introduction of fertilisers in the first half of the last century many areas have been ploughed and planted with crops. However sheep grazing does continue in places and, in others, a characteristic sight is immaculately managed grass tracks, the gallops used for training racehorses. The excellent turf of the downs makes this prime horse country but you need to be up early to see the strings of racehorses exercising.

At Streatley The Ridgeway crosses the River Thames and another of England's National Trails, the Thames Path, and enters more intimate and less open countryside. It follows the bank of the River Thames along a lovely 5 miles (8km) rural stretch before heading eastwards into the Chiltern Hills. Mostly on narrower paths, the Trail passes through woodlands, many of them beech, over neatly cultivated fields and across chalk grassland nature reserves rich in wildflowers. In contrast to the western half, although its usually peaceful here, you're never far from pleasant small towns or attractive villages.

With the support of Natural England, The Ridgeway is managed to the highest standards necessary for one of the most important paths in the country by the local highway authorities with a small dedicated team of staff and local volunteers.

Sheep on Pitstone Hill, Buckinghamshire

HISTORY II

For thousands of years, at least 5,000 and maybe many more, people have walked or ridden The Ridgeway, be they drovers, traders, invaders or today's recreational visitors. As part of a prehistoric track once stretching about 250 miles (400km) from the Dorset coast to the Wash on the Norfolk coast, The Ridgeway provided a route over the high ground for travellers which was less wooded and drier than routes through the springline villages below.

New Stone Age men, the first farmers in Britain, left the earliest remains. Their long barrows can be found at a few places both west and east of the River Thames. It was Bronze Age people from later times, around 2,000 BC, however, who dragged the huge sarsen stones from the surrounding hills and formed the dramatic Avebury Circle. There are many of their round burial barrows along the length of the National Trail.

Hill forts built during the Iron Age from about 500 BC until the Romans arrived in 43 AD are also found both sides of the Thames. These forts command the high ground and in several places they defended The Ridgeway against attack from the north.

In the Dark Ages The Ridgeway was a main route for the Saxons and Vikings who fought many battles during their advances into Wessex. In medieval times it was drovers driving livestock from Wales and the West Country to the Home Counties, not armies, who used The Ridgeway.

Until the Enclosure Acts of 1750 The Ridgeway was a broad band of tracks along the crest of the downs where travellers chose the driest or most convenient path. During Enclosures the exact course and width of The Ridgeway was defined by the building of earth banks and the planting of thorn hedges to prevent livestock straying into the newly cultivated fields.

In recent times use of The Ridgeway has changed greatly: farmers do still use much of it as an access route to their fields for tractors and other machinery but its main use is no longer utilitarian but recreational with walkers and riders out for exercise, pleasure and spiritual refreshment.

Avebury stones

III WILDLIFE

The grasslands which occur on the chalk of the downs and the Chilterns are some of the most interesting habitats in England and some of the richest in terms of the number of plant species found. Chalk grassland has suffered from modern farming and much has disappeared under the plough. However those unimproved chalk grassland areas along The Ridgeway, especially the nature reserves east of the Thames, are well worth visiting where you'll find, amongst many other lovely plants, several types of orchid.

Another botanical treat in store for visitors during springtime is the carpet of bluebells in many of the woodlands in the Chilterns, usually in the first couple of weeks of May.

For those keen on seeing birds, The Ridgeway should not disappoint you. A range of relatively common birds such as warblers and finches are found the length of The Ridgeway enjoying the food supply provided by the hedges lining the Trail. Skylarks, yellowhammers and corn buntings are particularly characteristic of the downland and although generally in decline in Britain are still fairly numerous along The Ridgeway. The song of the corn bunting, likened to the sound of a jangle of keys, is the distinctive sound of the western half of The Ridgeway.

In colder months flocks of redwing and fieldfare, winter visitors from Scandinavia, are common and are usually seen feeding in the fields surrounding the Trail. However, most people will especially cherish the site of a red kite and you'll be unlucky if you don't see one in the Chiltern Hills and increasingly west of the Thames too. These magnificent birds of prey recognised by their forked tail were reintroduced to this area in the late 1980s and are now well established. In woodlands of this area too, woodpeckers and nuthatches may well be spotted.

Apart from the ubiquitous rabbit, hares and deer are the larger wild animals you may encounter. Hares are found in open countryside and are bigger than rabbits with longer ears and hind legs. They are solitary animals and most active at night, so late evening or early morning are the best times to see them. Two species of deer are found on The Ridgeway, roe and fallow with the former being the smaller and also living in smaller groups of just three or four animals. Both of these species are nocturnal and shy so, as for hares, being on The Ridgeway at dusk or dawn will give you the best chance of viewing them.

WHO CAN USE THE RIDGEWAY? IV

Walkers

Walkers can use the whole length of the Trail. There are also a series of circular walks available that use sections of The Ridgeway - details on Ridgeway website.

Cyclists and Horseriders

Riders, both cyclists and horseriders, can share The Ridgeway with walkers all the way from the start at Overton Hill near Avebury to Streatley on the River Thames, a distance of roughly 43 miles (68km). Once across the river the only long section of the Trail which can be ridden is the 8-miles (13-km) stretch which follows the Icknield Way through the Chilterns from Britwell Hill near Watlington to Wainhill on the Oxfordshire/Buckinghamshire border. In other places The Ridgeway is a footpath and it is a trespass offence to ride on a footpath without the permission of the landowner.

However an alternative for riders is to join the Swan's Way long distance bridleway at Goring-on-Thames, just across the river from Streatley, and to follow this mostly on The Ridgeway to Bledlow west of Princes Risborough (here the Swan's Way turns north). From Bledlow riders can pick up the Icknield Way Riders' Route which provides a good alternative to The Ridgeway for riders as far as Pitstone Hill, just a couple of kilometres from Ivinghoe Beacon. Unfortunately riders can't continue to Ivinghoe Beacon, the official end of the National Trail, since the route to it is on footpaths.

There are some circular rides for cyclists and horseriders that use sections of The Ridgeway - details on Ridgeway website.

Vehicles

Recreational vehicles can now only use about 20% (17 miles) of The Ridgeway and, apart from two short sections, only from May until the end of September each year.

V PREPARING FOR YOUR VISIT

Deciding where to start

The Ridgeway can be walked in either direction and is signposted both ways. The route is generally promoted from west to east, starting at Overton Hill and finishing on Ivinghoe Beacon, because prevailing winds tend to come from the southwest and so will be behind you.

How far to walk in a day

How far you walk in a day is obviously up to you and will depend on your fitness and experience. As a guide, people generally walk at about 2½ miles (4km) an hour but on sections with climbs and descents slightly longer should be allowed. If you are planning to walk the whole length of The Ridgeway, or for several days, it is usually sensible to plan a short first day to ease yourself in gently.

What to take with you

- Carry warm and waterproof clothing as even on some summer days wind and rain can make a walk or ride uncomfortable.
- Walkers should wear strong, comfortable footwear. During the summer trainers are usually OK for a walk on The Ridgeway, but during wet periods and winter months wear walking boots or even Wellingtons if you're comfortable walking in these. Take a blister repair kit, just in case.
- Wear protection (hat and lotion) against the sun during the summer – the western half of the Trail is particularly exposed.
- Carry water if walking or riding for more than a couple of hours – water points west of the River Thames are relatively infrequent.
- If your walk or ride is along unfamiliar paths don't forget your map and/or guidebook!

Personal safety

If you are walking/riding alone it's sensible, as a simple precaution, to let someone know where you are and when you expect to arrive/return. Do bear in mind that mobile phone coverage can be patchy in rural areas, so you cannot always rely on it.

Dog Matters

If you are planning to undertake a long distance walk along The Ridgeway with your dog, you are advised to ensure it is fit before you start; on occasions walkers have had to abandon a walk because their dogs can't keep up! There are wax products available for applying to dogs' pads to help prevent soreness ... they might be worth investigating.

Please also make sure your dog is under close control at all times to prevent it from disturbing livestock or wildlife. You are asked to keep your dog on a lead when you're in the few fields you'll encounter with livestock, although if you find that cattle seriously harass you because of the dog, it's wise to let it off the lead.

VI HOW TO FOLLOW THE TRAIL

The Official National Trail Guide

The Ridgeway National Trail Guide by Anthony Burton, Aurum Press 2011. The official guide to the Trail with written route descriptions and colour 1:25,000 Ordnance Survey maps. Costs £12.99 and is available from the National Trails Office (see page 16).

Other Guides

Details of other guides and publications are on page 14.

Maps

It's usually a good idea to use maps when walking, particularly in unfamiliar areas. The official National Trail Guide includes colour sections of all the appropriate 1:25 000 Ordnance Survey maps needed to follow The Ridgeway. Alternatively, for you to enjoy and interpret the wider landscape, you may wish to purchase your own Ordnance Survey maps.

The Landranger series (pink cover at 1:50 000 or 2cm to 1km) has all public rights of way, viewpoints, tourist information and selected places of interest marked on them. For the whole of The Ridgeway you will need:

173 Swindon and Devizes
174 Newbury and Wantage
175 Reading and Windsor
165 Aylesbury and Leighton Buzzard

The larger scale Explorer series (orange cover at 1:25 000 or 4cm to 1km) has more detail including fence lines which can be very helpful when following rights of way, recreational routes and greater tourist information. For the whole of The Ridgeway you will need:

157 Marlborough and Savernake Forest
170 Abingdon, Wantage and Vale of White Horse
171 Chiltern Hills West
181 Chiltern Hills North

Signage

The Ridgeway follows a series of well-signed public rights of way and minor roads (91% of the Trail is off road).

The acorn is the symbol of National Trails and is used on all Ridgeway signage.

In most cases the signs, or waymark discs on gates or posts, will also carry the word 'Ridgeway'. The status of the right of way, which defines who can use it, will also be shown either in words, or by using the national waymarking scheme of coloured arrows – see below:

Footpath 

Bridleway 

Restricted Byway 

Byway 

The downs near Wantage

VII PUBLICATIONS

Publications About The Ridgeway

**Available from National Trails Office,* *see page 16*

The Ridgeway National Trail Guide* by Anthony Burton, Aurum Press 2011 - the official guide with written route descriptions from Overton Hill to Ivinghoe Beacon and colour 1:25 000 maps.

Ridgeway* Harvey Maps, 2008 - 1:40 000 scale waterproof map of The Ridgeway including information on a range of facilities along the Trail.

The Ridgeway: Avebury to Ivinghoe Beacon by Nick Hill, Trailblazer Publications, 2009.

Exploring the Ridgeway by Alan Charles, Countryside Books 2000 - based on 14 circular walks covering The Ridgeway from Ivinghoe Beacon to Overton Hill.

The Oldest Road - an Exploration of the Ridgeway by J R L Anderson with photographs by Fay Godwin. Paperback edition by Whittet Books, 1992.

Walking in Britain, Lonely Planet, 2007 - includes a description of the western half of The Ridgeway.

The Greater Ridgeway by Ray Quinlan, Cicerone, 2003. Describes a route from Lyme Regis to Hunstanton, including The Ridgeway National Trail.

Let's Hear it for The Ridgeway!* by Elizabeth Newbery - a family activity book full of ideas and information on things to do and see on and close to The Ridgeway.

TOUR OPERATORS & BAGGAGE TRANSFER VIII

The following companies offer self-guided or guided holiday packages on part or all of The Ridgeway.

Walking

Celtic Trails Walking Holidays T: 01291 689774 www.celtic-trails.com/englandwalkingholidays/theridgeway

Contours Walking Holidays T: 01629 821900 www.contours.co.uk

Discovery Travel T: 01904 632226 www.discoverytravel.co.uk/trips/ridgeway

Explore Britain T: 01740 650900 www.explorebritain.com

Freedom Walking Holidays T: 01491 872227 www.freedomwalkingholidays.co.uk

Macs Adventure T: 0141 530 8886 www.macsadventure.com

Baggage Transfer

Carrier Bags T: 01491 871111 www.ridgewaytransportation.co.uk - weekend or day tour including part of The Ridgeway.

Accommodation Providers Many will transport your luggage to your next night's accommodation.

Cycling

History on Your Handlebars T: 01249 730013 www.historyonyourhandlebars.co.uk - weekend or day tour including part of The Ridgeway.

Horse Riding

Pewsey Vale Riding Centre, Church Farm, Stanton St Bernard, Marlborough SN8 4LJ **T:** 01672 851400 - www.pewseyvaleridingcentre.com - 1 or 2-day ride from Pewsey to Streatley.

Redlands Equestrian T: 01225 424413 www.redlandsequestrian.com

IX USEFUL CONTACTS

The Ridgeway Managers and National Trails Office

Margaret Caddick and Jos Joslin, National Trails Office, Signal Court, Old Station Way, Eynsham OX29 4TL. **T**: 01865 810224.
E: Nationaltrails@oxfordshire.gov.uk

Highway Authorities responsible for public rights of way

Buckinghamshire County Council **T**: 0845 370 8090 www.buckscc.gov.uk

Hertfordshire County Council **T**: 0300 123 4040 www.hertsdirect.org

Oxfordshire County Council **T**: 01865 810226 www.oxfordshire.gov.uk

Swindon Borough Council **T**: 01793 445500 www.swindon.gov.uk

West Berkshire Council **T**: 01635 519080 www.westberks.gov.uk

Wiltshire Council **T**: 0300 456 0100 www.wiltshire.gov.uk

Agency responsible for National Trails

Natural England **T**: 0300 060 1904 www.naturalengland.org.uk

Areas of Outstanding Natural Beauty

North Wessex Downs AONB **T**: 01488 685440 www.northwessexdowns.org.uk

Chilterns AONB **T**: 01844 355500 www.chilternsaonb.org

Organisations for walkers

Backpackers Club - www.backpackersclub.co.uk

Long Distance Walkers Association - www.ldwa.org.uk

Oxford Fieldpaths Society - www.ofs.org.uk

Ramblers Association **T**: 020 7339 8500 www.ramblers.org.uk

Organisations for cyclists

British Cycling Federation **T**: 0161 274 2000 www.britishcycling.org.uk

Cyclists Touring Club (Off-Road) **T**: 01483 238337 www.ctc.org.uk

Sustrans **T**: 0845 113 0065 www.sustrans.org.uk

The Rough Stuff Fellowship **T**: 01457 852090 www.rsf.org.uk

Organisations for horseriders

British Horse Society **T**: 0844 848 1666 www.bhs.org.uk

Byways & Bridleways Trust - www.bbtrust.org.uk

Endurance GB **T**: 02476 697929 www.endurancegb.co.uk

Tourist Information providers

Details of these are included in the introductory pages to each of the six sections of The Ridgeway.

Other organisations

Berkshire, Buckinghamshire & Oxfordshire Wildlife Trust **T**: 01865 775476 www.bbowt.org.uk

Chiltern Society **T**: 01494 771250 www.chilternsociety.org.uk

Friends of the Ridgeway - www.ridgewayfriends.org.uk

Herts & Middlesex Wildlife Trust **T**: 01727 858901 www.hertswildlifetrust.org.uk

Wiltshire Wildlife Trust **T**: 01380 725670 www.wiltshirewildlife.org

X GETTING THERE

Getting to The Ridgeway by public transport is fairly easy, particularly the eastern half of the Trail. Visit our website www.nationaltrail.co.uk/ridgeway to find a map-based online travel planner with information on train and bus services.

Alternatively, telephone numbers and websites to find out more about public transport to the Trail are listed below:

• Rail Services	08457 484950 (24 hours a day) www.nationalrail.co.uk
• Bus Services	0871 2002233 www.traveline.info
• Taxi Services	Information is included in each of the six sections

We encourage people to consider using public transport rather than travelling by private car as this is better for the environment, helps to support local public transport services and reduces congestion from parking in the smaller settlements. However, those wishing to travel to The Ridgeway by car are asked to park considerately if parking in villages on or close to the Trail. Other places to park are listed within each section.

FOLLOW THE COUNTRYSIDE CODE XI

- **Be safe – plan ahead and follow any signs**

Even when going out locally, it's best to get the latest information about where and when you can go. Follow advice and local signs, and be prepared for the unexpected.

- **Leave gates and property as you find them**

Please respect the working life of the countryside, as our actions can affect people's livelihoods, our heritage, and the safety and welfare of animals and ourselves.

- **Protect plants and animals, and take your litter home**

We have a responsibility to protect our countryside now and for future generations, so make sure you don't harm animals, birds, plants or trees.

- **Keep your dog under close control**

The countryside is a great place to exercise dogs, but it's every owner's duty to make sure their dog is not a danger or nuisance to farm animals, wildlife or other people.

- **Consider other people**

Showing consideration and respect for other people makes the countryside a pleasant environment for everyone – at home, at work and at leisure.

For further details visit www.countrysideaccess.gov.uk

XII EMERGENCY CONTACTS

We hope you will not need to refer to this page during your visit but the information below will help you find the service you need quickly should something unforeseen occur. In urgent and life threatening situations, or when a crime is in progress, the emergency services can be contacted on **999 or 112**.

When the situation is not an emergency please use the following contact details:

Police

To contact local police stations dial 101

Hospitals

The following hospitals with casualty departments are located in the places shown below. The telephone numbers given are the hospital switchboard; ask to be put through to Accident and Emergency Reception.

◆ Full 24-hour emergency service

▲ Minor injuries only, NOT 24-hour service

Section	Town	Telephone No	Address
1&2	◆ Swindon	01793 604020	The Great Western Hospital, Marlborough Road, Swindon SN3 6BB
3&4	▲ Abingdon	01235 208730	Abingdon Community Hospital, Marcham Road, Abingdon OX14 1AG
3&4	◆ Oxford	01865 741166	John Radcliffe Hospital Headley Way, Headington Oxford OX3 9DU
3&4	▲ Wallingford	01865 425200	Wallingford Community Hospital, Reading Road, Wallingford OX10 9DU (Mon-Fri 8:30-18:30)
5&6	◆ Aylesbury	01296 315000	Stoke Mandeville Hospital, Mandeville Road, Aylesbury HP21 8AL

ACCOMMODATION, FACILITIES & SERVICES XIII

The following chapters give details of the settlements, accommodation, eating places, shops, attractions and other facilities along or near The Ridgeway. They are listed in geographic order from Overton Hill to Ivinghoe Beacon.

If you fail to find accommodation using this guide please contact the Visitor Information Centre listed near the beginning of each section which may be able to provide other addresses.

To find map grid references for individual accommodation put postcodes into www.nearby.org.uk

You are strongly advised to book accommodation in advance. Whilst booking, do check prices since those quoted here are usually the minimum charged. It's also wise to book evening meals in advance if eating in village pubs as they can get very busy.

For those who would like to enjoy more than a day on The Ridgeway without having to carry all their possessions, many accommodation providers have indicated whether they are willing to transport the luggage you don't need during the day to your next night's accommodation. The fee charged for this service needs to be discussed and agreed at the time of the booking. Accommodation providers have also indicated if they are willing to collect you from The Ridgeway and deliver you back after your stay.

All the information within this Companion is as accurate as possible. Inclusion of accommodation does not constitute a recommendation although it is indicated in the details whether an establishment has a recognised grade awarded to it. If you have any comments or notice any errors, please write to Jos Joslin the National Trails Manager (page 16).

Camping on The Ridgeway

The situation regarding camping on The Ridgeway is, in theory, clear enough; The Ridgeway is privately owned and the public right of way along it is for passage only, not for stopping and camping.

In practice, however, most landowners do not object if a tent is pitched on The Ridgeway for a night and disappears the next morning as long as no litter is left, no damage done, nor camp fires lit. Do not camp in adjoining fields, woods or gallops without prior permission from the landowner

XIII ACCOMMODATION, FACILITIES & SERVICES

Key to Symbols for Settlements

Any comments relate to preceding icon

map grid reference (see start of each section for relevant maps)

shortest walking distance from The Ridgeway

most convenient train station

P£ car park (paying)

PF car park (free)

toilets

WC toilets adapted for disabled users

Visitor Information Centre

pub (usually open lunchtimes 11am-3pm then evenings 6pm-11pm). Names and telephone numbers of pubs are given for those settlements with up to two pubs

bar meals in pub

post office (usual opening hours 9am-5.30pm weekdays; 9:00-12.30pm Sat)

general store (usual opening hours daily 9am-5.30pm Mon-Sat)

cafe/tea shop

restaurant

food take-away

opening hours of services relate to the preceding symbol

S M T W T F S

eg:

open all day

closed all day

Post offices, general stores, cafe/tea shops - open morning; Pubs, bar meals, restaurants, takeaways - open lunchtime

Post offices, general stores, cafe/tea shops - open afternoon; Pubs, bar meals, restaurants, takeaways - open evening

£ bank (usually open daily 9.30am-4.30pm Mon-Fri)

cash machine available, including outside bank opening hours

tourist attraction

Key to Symbols for Accommodation

Type of accommodation (symbols in margins)

▲	hostel	B&B	bed and breakfast
	camping		horse accommodation
	hotel	SC	self catering
	inn		

The Plough, Lower Cadsden

XIII ACCOMMODATION, FACILITIES & SERVICES

The number and price following the symbols for rooms gives the number and price of that type of room available. The same applies to tent/caravan pitches and stabling/grazing for horses. Prices quoted for rooms are the minimum price per room per night for bed and breakfast. The price for single occupancy of double or twin is given in brackets eg (£35.00).

Accommodation symbols - hotels, inns, guest houses, B&Bs and hostels

- double room
- twin room
- family room
- single room
- children welcome
- wheelchair access
- dogs allowed by arrangement
- V caters for vegetarians
- most food locally produced
- some food locally produced
- most food is organic
- some food is organic
- packed lunches available
- evening meals available by arrangement
- grazing for horses
- stabling for horses
- secure cycle storage
- DRY clothes/boots drying facilities
- laundry facilities
- transport to and from Trail by arrangement
- luggage transported to next overnight stop by arrangement
- credit card(s) accepted
- ★ VisitBritain accommodation standard
- special feature/comment

Accommodation symbols - camping and caravan sites

- tent pitches
- caravan pitches
- cold water
- hot water
- toilets
- WC toilets adapted for disabled users
- showers
- secure cycle storage
- laundry facilities
- site shop
- CG camping gas
- special feature/comment

Section 1

Overton Hill to Ogbourne St George

Starting in the Avebury World Heritage Site with its wealth of archaeology, this 9.3 miles (14.8km) stretch of The Ridgeway climbs gradually to a high point at Barbury Castle Iron Age fort. From there the route along Smeathe's Ridge provides great views on either side as it gently descends to the valley of the River Og.

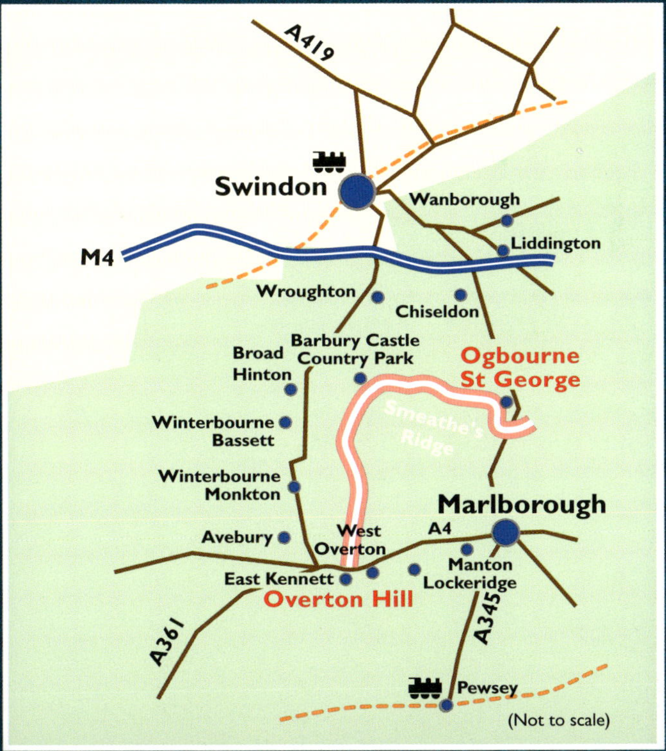

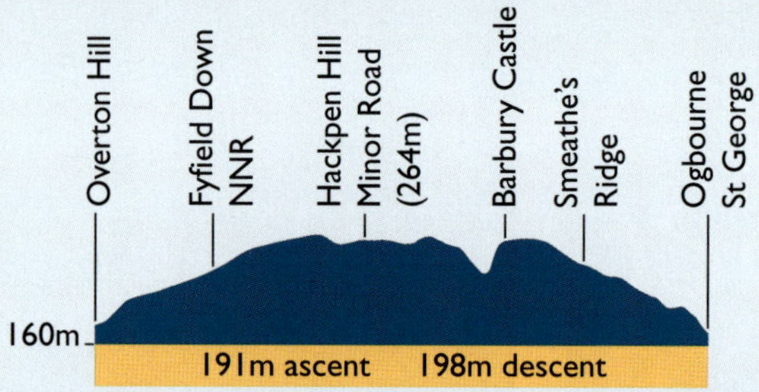

Maps

Landranger maps	173	Swindon and Devizes
Explorer maps	157	Marlborough and Savernake Forest

Taxis

Place	Name	Telephone Number
Marlborough	Arrow Private Hire	01672 515567
	Kayze Cars	01672 514556
	Marlborough Taxis	01672 512786
	Paddy's Taxis	01672 511884

Car Parking

If you choose to park in villages close to The Ridgeway, please park considerately. Other places to park are listed below but you need to be aware that theft from cars parked in the countryside does occur. You are advised to leave any unnecessary items at home or, failing that, ensure that anything valuable is locked in the boot of your vehicle.

Place	Map Grid Reference
On Ridgeway at the start at Overton Hill, on north side of A4, 4 1/2 miles (7km) west of Marlborough	SU 119681
On Ridgeway at Hackpen Hill on minor road between Marlborough and Broad Hinton, 2 miles (3km) east of Broad Hinton	SU 129747
On Ridgeway at Barbury Castle Country Park, 5 miles (8km) south of Swindon signed from Wroughton and Chiseldon	SU 157762

Water Points

Place	Map Grid Reference
Elm Tree Cottage, Southend (please ask before using)	SU 198734

Toilets

Place	Map Grid Reference
Barbury Castle Country Park	SU 155762

Vets

Place	Name	Telephone Number
Marlborough	The Drove Veterinary Hospital	01672 512043
	Riverside Veterinary Centre	01672 514875

Farriers

Place	Name	Telephone Number
Marlborough	J Baker	01672 514013
	I Buck	07702 512288
	AP Marshall	07053 518057
	ND Quinlan	07912 566780
	AJ Turnell	07768 535271
Aldbourne	Peter Baker	01672 540812
Wroughton	P A Groom	01793 814185

Saddlers

Place	Name	Telephone Number
Marlborough	G & S Saddlery	01672 569288
Tockenham, Swindon	Old Dairy Saddlery	01793 849284

Riding Stables for Guided Rides

Place	Name	Telephone Number
Marlborough	Pewsey Vale Riding Centre	01672 851400
Chiseldon	Ladysmith Equestrian Centre	01793 740842

Horsebox Parking

The following places have sufficient space for you to park your horsebox. You **must** call in advance to arrange as space may be scarce. A fee may also be charged.

Place	Name	Telephone Number
Marlborough	Brown's Farm (Accommodation guests and day-riders)	01672 515129
Ogbourne St George	Foxlynch (Accommodation guests and day-riders)	01672 841307

Bike Repairs

Place	Name	Telephone Number
Marlborough	Acceler8 Cycles	01672 513414
	Bertie Maffoons	01672 519119
Swindon	Bike Doctor	01793 874873
	Dans Cycles	01793 423380
	Mitchell Cycles	01793 523306
	Swindon Cycles Superstore	01793 700105
	Total Bike	01793 644185

Mountain Bike Hire

Place	Name	Telephone Number
Swindon	Swindon Cycles Superstore	01793 700105

Visitor Information Centres

These VICs are staffed but note that many libraries in the area also have leaflets about local attractions and events.

★ offers accommodation booking service

Place	**Address/Opening Hours**
Avebury & Marlborough	**T**: 01672 539179 www.visitwiltshire.co.uk Opening hours: Summer (April-Oct) Daily 9:30-17:00 Winter (Nov-Mar) Thur-Sun 9:30-16:30
★ Swindon	Central Library, Regents Circus, Swindon SN1 1QG **T**: 01793 466454 **E**: infocentre@swindon.gov.uk www.visitwiltshire.co.uk/swindon Opening hours: All year: Mon-Sat 10:00-16:00

Autumn ploughing

Marlborough

SU1969 4.4 miles (7km)
Pusey 6.9 miles (11.1 km)

Town with full range of services. Visit www.marlboroughwiltshire.co.uk for further details, including information about a range of accommodation.

&B SC

Browns Farm

GR SU198678 0.9miles(1.5km) south of Marlborough
Mrs Hazel I Crockford
Browns Farm, Marlborough SN8 4ND
T: 01672 515129 **M:** 07931 311985
E: crockford@farming.co.uk
www. marlboroughholidaycottages.co.
1 £50 1 £45 (£30) 1 £65
V DRY
Most major cards. Some rooms en-suite
2 £10 4 £10
Free WiFi in B&B. 3 self contained properties for self-catering also available from £200/week ★★★ Horsebox parking available for day-riders

Postern Hill Camping & Caravan Site

Proprietor
Postern Hill, Marlborough
SN8 4ND
T: 01672 515195
or 170 £8/pitch
No toilets during winter months

Manton

SU1768 4.1 miles (6.6km) avoiding main road
Pewsey 6 miles (9.7km)

S M T W T F S S M T W T F S

Pub: Outside Chance 01672 512352

Beech Hill

B&B

Mrs Elizabeth Bonham
Manton Drove, Manton, Marlborough
SN8 4HL
T: 01672 519833
E: liz.bonham@virgin.net
www.beechhillhouse.net
3 £80 (£50) V DRY All rooms ensuite

Lockeridge

SU1467 1.6 miles (2.5km)
Pewsey 7.1 miles (11.4km)

S M T W T F S S M T W T F S

Pub: Who'd A Thought It Inn 01672 861255

Taffrail

closed Dec B&B

Mrs Julie Spencer
Back Lane, Lockeridge, Marlborough
SN8 4ED
T/F: 01672 861266
E: spencer@taffrail.eclipse.co.uk
1 £50 2 £50 (£30) (min age 8) V DRY

West Overton

SU1367 0.6 miles (1km)
Pewsey 8.5 miles (13.6km)

S M T W T F S   S M T W T F S

Pub: Bell Inn 01672 861099

East Kennett

SU1267 0.4 miles (0.7km)
Pewsey 11 miles (18km)

B&B **Old Forge**

Mrs Laura Feeley
East Kennett, Marlborough SN8 4EY
T: 01672 861686 **M:** 07770 871066
E: laura@feeleyfamily.fsnet.co.uk
www.theoldforge-avebury.co.uk
2 £70 1 £75 (£55) 1 £80 V
Visa, Mastercard ★★★★ Some rooms en-suite
VisitBritain Gold Award

Avebury

SU1069 1.2 miles (2km)
Pewsey 10.6 miles (17km) PF
WC

S M T W T F S   S M T W T F S

S M T W T F S   S M T W T F S

S M T W T F S

Pub: Red Lion 01672 539266

☆ Avebury World Heritage Site
T: 01672 539250
www.nationaltrust.org.uk

☆ Alexander Keiller Museum
T: 0117 975 0700
www.nationaltrust.org.uk

Manor Farm *closed Xmas & Easter* B&B

Mrs Judith Farthing
High Street, Avebury, Marlborough
SN8 1RF
T: 01672 539294
www.manorfarmavebury.com
1 £85 1 £85 (£75) (min age 12) V ★★★★
Private bathroom

B&B **Avebury Life**

Antoinette Kremer
5 Trusloe Cottages, Avebury Trusloe,
Marlborough SN8 1QZ
T: 01672 539644 **M:** 07788 443632
E: info@aveburylife.com
www.aveburylife.com
/ 1 £70 (£45) 1 £40
V Double room en-suite
Single room has separate bathroom

B&B **Avebury Lodge** *closed 25th & 26th Dec*

Mr Andrew Blackall
The Lodge, High Street, Avebury,
Marlborough SN8 1RF
T: 01672 539023
E: avebury@email.com
www.aveburylodge.co.uk
2 £150 1 £175 (£120) 1£250 V
Mastercard, Visa. Some rooms en-suite
This is a vegetarian B&B. WiFi in rooms

B&B **Silbury Hill View** *closed Nov-end Feb*

Mrs Denise Dixon
6 Beckhampton Road, Avebury,
Marlborough SN8 1QT
T: 01672 539588
2 £60 1 £60 (£40) (min age 8) V

Winterbourne Monkton

SU1072 1.9 miles (3km)
Swindon 10.3 miles (16.5km)
PF

S M T W T F S   S M T W T F S

Pub: New Inn 01672 539240

New Inn *closed Xmas & New Year*

Mrs Sandra Pope
The New Inn, Winterbourne Monkton,
Swindon SN4 9NW
T. 01672 539240
E: enquiries@thenewinn.net
www.thenewinn.net
2 £60 2 £60 1 £70 1 £50 V DRY
Most major cards. All rooms en-suite.
Evening meals not available Sunday, Monday and Tuesday

Winterbourne Bassett

SU1075 1.9 miles (3km)
Swindon 8 miles (13km)

S M T W T F S   S M T W T F S

Pub: White Horse Inn 01793 731257

Broad Hinton

SU1076 1.9 miles (3km)
Swindon 7 miles (11km)

S M T W T F S S M T W T F S
S M T W T F S S M T W T F S

in Post Office
Pubs: Crown Inn 01793 731302 & Barbury Inn 01793 731510

B&B **Compton Farmhouse**

Mrs Helen Tulissio
Summers Road, Broad Hinton SN4 9PA
T: 01793 739278 **M:** 07768 892240
E: info@comptonfarmhouse.com
www.comptonfarmhouse.com
1 £100 (£75) V DRY Most major cards.
★★★★★ Room is en-suite.
Room is a luxury suite for up to 4 people

Wroughton

SU1480 2.7 miles (4.3km)
Swindon 3.8 miles (6.1km) PF

Large village with range of services
☆ Wroughton Science Museum
T: 020 7942 4000
www.sciencemuseum.org.uk/wroughton

Overtown Manor B&B

Mrs Nancy Lawson
Wroughton, Swindon SN4 0SH
T: 01793 814737 **M:** 07887 597090
E: nancy@overtownmanor.co.uk
www. overtownmanor.co.uk
/ 3 £95 (£65) (min age10)
V O DRY
Most major cards ★★★★★ All rooms en-suite
VisitBritain Silver Award.

Barbury Castle from The Ridgeway

CHISELDON

SU1879 1.9 miles (3km)
Swindon 5 miles (8km) PF

S M T W T F S S M T W T F S
S M T W T F S S M T W T F S

In petrol station
Pubs: Patriots Arms 01793 740331 & Plough Inn 01793 740342
☆ Chiseldon Museum **T:** 01793 740784

B&B Courtleigh House

Mrs Ruth Hibberd
40 Draycott Road, Chiseldon, Swindon
SN4 0LS
T: 01793 740246 **M:** 07896 296909
E: courtleighhouse@yahoo.co.uk
www.courtleighhouse.co.uk
1 £80 1 £80 (£40) (min age1) V DRY
★★★★ Some rooms en-suite
VisitBritain Silver Award. Lift available to pub for evening meal

B&B Rossendale

Mrs Anne Wirdnam
44a Station Road, Chiseldon, Swindon
SN6 0PW
T: 01793 740726
E: anne@rossendale.biz
www.rossendale.biz
1 £70 1 £65 (£45) 1 £85 1 £40 V DRY
★★★★ Some rooms en-suite

Chiseldon House Hotel

Mrs Sue Higgs
New Road, Chiseldon, Swindon
SN4 0NE
T: 01793 741010
E: welcome@chiseldonhouse.com
www.chiseldonhouse.com
15 £80 5 £80 1 £65 V DRY Most major cards ★★★ All rooms en-suite

Patriots Arms

Mrs Lena Sands
6 New Road, Chiseldon, Swindon
SN4 0LU
T: 01793 740331
E: lena@patriotsarms.co.uk
www.patriotsarms.co.uk
2 £50 Most major cards. All rooms en-suite
Breakfast taken in room – cereal/tea/coffee only

Crab apple

Ogbourne St George

SU2074 0.6 miles (1km)
Swindon 8 miles (13km)

S M T W T F S   S M T W T F S

Pubs: Inn With The Well 01672 841445 & Parklands Hotel 01672 841555

B&B **Sanctuary**

Mrs Rebecca MacDonald
Ogbourne St George, Marlborough SN8 1SQ
T: 01672 841473
E: bandb@the-sanctuary.biz
www.the-sanctuary.biz
1 £70 1 £70 (£53) 1 £87
DRY
★★★★ Some rooms en-suite

INN **Inn with the Well**

Mr Michael Shaw
Marlborough Road, Ogbourne St George, Marlborough SN8 1SQ
T: 01672 841445
E: info@theinnwiththewell.co.uk
www.theinnwiththewell.co.uk
3 £65 2 £65 (£57) 1 £85
VISA
Most major cards ★★★ All rooms en-suite
No evening meals Sundays October to March

Foxlynch B&B

Mr G Edwins
Ogbourne St George, Marlborough
SN8 1TD
T: 01672 841307 **M:** 07855 909882
Bunkroom £20/person
20 £5/person 6 £5/person
DRY
4 £12 4 £12
Fee charged for transport to/from Ridgeway. Horsebox parking available for guests and day riders £5 per day

Lavender House B&B

Mrs Jane Shave
High Street, Ogbourne St George, Marlborough SN8 1SL
M: 07725 324869
E: lavenderhouse53@yahoo.com
1 £65 1 £60 (£40) 1 £30
DRY
Some rooms en-suite

Parklands Hotel H

Mr Mark Bentley
Ogbourne St George, Marlborough SN8 1SL
T: 01672 841555
E: mark@parklandshoteluk.co.uk
www.parklandshoteluk.co.uk
/ 11 £79 (£59) 1 £95
(min age 8) DRY
VISA Most major cards. All rooms en-suite

Section 2

Ogbourne St George to Sparsholt Firs

Probably the most remote section of The Ridgeway, this 16 miles (25.6km) runs along the scarp face of the downs passing two Iron Age forts at Liddington and Uffington, the Stone Age long barrow of Wayland's Smithy and the wonderful figure of the Uffington White Horse. It also passes the only pub, at Fox Hill, directly on the western half of the Trail!

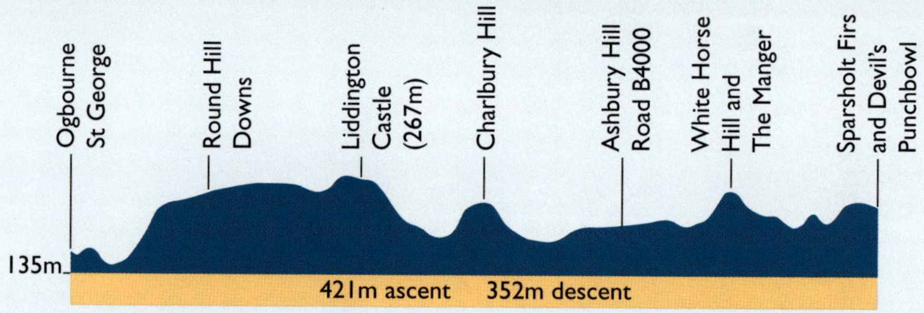

Maps

Landranger maps	174	Newbury and Wantage
Explorer maps	157	Marlborough and Savernake Forest
	170	Abingdon, Wantage and Vale of White Horse

Taxis

Place	**Name**	**Telephone Number**
Lambourn	Ray's	01488 71819
Childrey	Berkeley Executive Cars	07775 647790
East Challow	Bonny's Taxis	07753 165890
Wantage	Cab Co	01235 772424
	Chapel Cars	07789 551931
	Evenlode Taxis	01235 762035
	Keith's of Wantage	01235 763344
	Stuart's Taxis	01235 770608
	Webb's of Wantage	07881 647777

Car Parking

If you choose to park in villages close to The Ridgeway, please park considerately. Other places to park are listed below but you need to be aware that theft from cars parked in the countryside does occur. You are advised to leave any unnecessary items at home or, failing that, ensure that anything valuable is locked in the boot of your vehicle.

Place	**Map Grid Reference**
On Ridgeway at Fox Hill near Wanborough, 200m north-east of Shepherds Rest on road to Hinton Parva	SU 233814
On Ridgeway ½ mile (1km) south of Ashbury on B4000	SU 274844
National Trust car park for Uffington White Horse, south off B4507, ½ mile (700m) north of The Ridgeway	SU 293866
On Ridgeway at Sparsholt Firs on the south side of B4001, 2½ miles (4km) south of Childrey	SU 344851

Water Points

* with troughs for animals

Place	Map Grid Reference
Elm Tree Cottage, Southend (please ask before using)	SU 198734
Idstone Barn, Ashbury* (summer only - this supply comes from a private reservoir and can be intermittent. Fill bottle immediately as it may run dry after a few seconds)	SU 263835
Hill Barn, Sparsholt Firs*	SU 338854

Vets

* large animal vets

Place	Name	Telephone Number
Swindon	Eastcott Veterinary Hospital	01793 528341
	The Drove Veterinary Hospital*	01793 522483
	Thameswood Veterinary Clinic	01793 511267
Lambourn	The Drove Veterinary Clinic	01488 71505
	Valley Equine Hospital*	01488 71999
Faringdon	Danetree Veterinary Surgeons	01367 242777
	Elms Veterinary Surgery	01367 242416
Wantage	Abivale Veterinary Group	01235 770333
	Danetree Veterinary Surgeons	01235 770227

Farriers

Place	Name	Telephone Number
Uffington	Mervyn Richings	01367 820253
Lambourn	Alex Campbell	07702 126620
	LA Cartmell	01488 71985
	Chapel Forge Farriers	01488 72613
	AJ Charles	07831 595073
Ashbury	Terry Gill	07765 407840

Saddlers

Place	Name	Telephone Number
Lambourn	E J Wicks	01488 71766
Goosey	Asti Equestrian	01367 710288
Challow Station	Horse Shoe Saddlery	01367 710797
Childrey	White Horse Animal Feeds (no tack)	01235 751529

Riding Stables for Guided Rides

Place	Name	Telephone Number
Lambourn	Folly Foot Stables	01488 71059
Hinton Parva	Charbury Farm Stables	01793 790065
Baulking	Baulking Grange	01367 718678
Kingston Lisle	Holistic Horses	01367 820033

Horsebox Parking

The following places have sufficient space for you to park your horsebox. You **must** call in advance to arrange as space may be scarce. A fee may also be charged.

Place	Name	Telephone Number
Sparsholt Down	Down Barn Farm (Accommodation guests and day-riders)	01367 820272
Sparsholt Firs	Hill Barn (Accommodation guests and day-riders)	01235 751236

Bike Repairs

Place	Name	Telephone Number
Swindon	Mitchell Cycles	01793 523306
	Swindon Cycles Superstore	01793 700105
	Bike Doctor	01793 874873
	Total Bike	01793 644185
Wantage	Ridgeway Cycles	01235 764445
	GMC	01235 764204

Mountain Bike Hire

Place	Name	Telephone Number
Swindon	Swindon Cycles Superstore	01793 700105

Visitor Information Centres

These VICs are staffed but note that many libraries in the area also have leaflets about local attractions and events.

★ offers accommodation booking service

Place	**Address/Opening Hours**
★ Swindon	Central Library, Regents Circus, Swindon SN1 1QG **T**: 01793 466454 **E**: infocentre@swindon.gov.uk www.visitwiltshire.co.uk/swindon Opening hours: All year: Mon-Sat 10:00-16:00
★ Faringdon	The Corn Exchange, Corn Market, Faringdon SN7 7JA **T**: 01367 242191 **E**: tic@faringdontowncouncil.gov.uk www.faringdontowncouncil.gov.uk Opening hours: Mon-Fri 9:00-14:00, Sat 9:30-13:00
★ Wantage	Vale and Downland Museum & Visitor Centre 19 Church Street, Wantage OX12 8BL **T**: 01235 771447 **E**: tourism@wantage-museum.com Opening hours: All year: Mon-Sat 10:00-16:00

East of White Horse Hill

Aldbourne

SU2675 3.3 miles (5.2km)
Swindon 10 miles (16km)
WC

S M T W T F S S M T W T F S

S M T W T F S S M T W T F S

in Post Office and Co-Op
Pubs: Blue Boar 01672 540237 &
Crown 01672 540214

Crown at Aldbourne

Mr Alan Walters
2 The Square, Aldbourne, Marlborough
SN8 2DU
T: 01672 540214 **M:** 07773 219579
E: booking@thecrownaldbourne.co.uk
www.thecrownaldbourne.co.uk
3 £70 1 £60 V Most major cards. All rooms en-suite

Liddington

SU2081 0.6 miles (1km)
Swindon 4 miles (7km)

S M T W T F S S M T W T F S

Pubs: Village Inn 01793 790314

☆ Liddington Castle
www.themodernantiquarian.com/site/3080

Wanborough

SU2182 1.2 miles (2km)
Swindon 4 miles (7km)

S M T W T F S S M T W T F S

S M T W T F S S M T W T F S

in Post Office

Great Moorleaze Farm B&B

Mrs Joanna Rees-Bains
The Marsh, Wanborough, Swindon
SN4 0SW
T: 01793 485838 **M:** 07976 879602
E: joannarees@aol.com
www.greatmoorleaze-farm.co.uk
5 £70 5 £35 V DRY All major cards. All rooms en-suite

Bishopstone

SU2483 0.6 miles (1km)
Swindon 7 miles (11km)

S M T W T F S S M T W T F S

Pubs: Royal Oak 01793 790481

Cheney Thatch *closed Xmas & New Year* B&B

Mrs R Boot
Oxon Place, Bishopstone, Swindon
SN6 8PS
T: 01793 790508
2 £50 (£40) (min age 10) V DRY ★★★ All rooms en-suite

B&B **Prebendal Farm** *closed Xmas & New Year*

Mrs Jo Selbourne
Bishopstone, Swindon SN6 8PT
T: 01793 790485 **E:** jo@prebendal.com
www.prebendal.com
3 £90 1 £90 (£50) V DRY Some rooms en-suite
Complimentary tea and cakes on arrival

Royal Oak INN

Mr Tim Finney
Cues Lane, Bishopstone, Swindon
SN6 8PP
T: 01793 790481
E: royaloak@helenbrowningorganics.co.uk
www.helenbrowningorganics.co.uk
1 £90 1 £90 V DRY Most major cards. All rooms en-suite
Room prices vary depending whether evening meal and/or breakfast taken. Book evening meal in advance. Most food provided is grown on our own organic farm.

Ashbury

SU2685 0.6 miles (1km)
Swindon 8 miles (13km)

S M T W T F S S M T W T F S

Pub: Rose & Crown Hotel 01793 710222

☆ Ashdown House
T: 01494 755569
www.nationaltrust.org.uk

Rose & Crown INN

Billy and Sandra Downes
The High Street, Ashbury, Swindon
SN6 8NA
T: 01793 710222
www.roseandcrownatashbury.co.uk
3 £48 3 £48 1 £48 V Most major cards. All rooms en-suite
Breakfast additional £5

Woolstone

SU2987 1.2 miles (2km)
Swindon 11 miles (18km)

S M T W T F S   S M T W T F S

Pub: White Horse Inn 01367 820726

White Horse

Mr Keith Adams
Woolstone, Faringdon SN7 7QL
T: 01367 820726 **M:** 07818 257154
E: info@whitehorsewoolstone.co.uk
www.whitehorsewoolstone.co.uk
4 £75 2 £75 (£60) 1 £130
V DRY
Most major cards ★★★ All rooms en-suite

Uffington

SU3089 1.9 miles (3km)
Swindon 12 miles (19km) PF

S M T W T F S   S M T W T F S

S M T W T F S   S M T W T F S

Open summer only
S M T W T F S

Pub: Fox & Hounds 01367 820680
☆ Tom Brown's School Museum
www.museum.uffington.net.html

☆ Uffington White Horse and Castle
T: 01793 762209
www.nationaltrust.org.uk

Norton House — closed Xmas — B&B

Mrs Fenella Oberman
Broad Street, Uffington, Faringdon SN7 7RA
T: 01367 820230
E: carloberman123@btinternet.com
www.smoothhound.co.uk/hotels/nortonfaringdon
1 £60 (£40) 1 £60 1 £35
V DRY
★★★★
VisitBritain Silver Award. Private bathrooms. Small charge for transport to/from Ridgeway

Britchcombe Countryside Holiday

SU307873 ½ mile from Ridgeway
Mrs Marcella Seymour
Britchcombe Farm, Uffington, Faringdon SN7 7QJ
T: 01367 821022 **M:** 07748 005362
E: marcella@seymour8227.freeserve.co.uk
£7/person £7/person
WC DRY
Yurt and tipi available for hire. Packed lunches can be provided

Kingston Lisle

SU3287 1.2 miles (2km)
Swindon 14 miles (22km)

S M T W T F S   S M T W T F S

Pub: Blowingstone Inn 01367 820288

Sparsholt

SU3487 1.9 miles (3km)
Didcot 12 miles (20km)

S M T W T F S   S M T W T F S

Pub: Star Inn 01235 751539 - pub for sale as Companion went to print, so check for opening times

Hill Barn Farmhouse B&B

SU338852 100m S of Ridgeway
Mrs Joanna Whittington
Sparsholt Firs, Wantage OX12 9XB
T: 01235 751236 **M:** 07885 368918
E: jmw@hillbarn.plus.com
www.hillbarnbedandbreakfast.co.uk
1 £75 1 £75 (£45) V
DRY ★★★ All rooms en-suite
5 £5/person
DRY
4 £15 4 £10
Free horsebox parking for guests and day riders

B&B **Down Barn Farm** *closed Xmas*

GR SU333851 900m S of Ridgeway

Mrs P A Reid
Sparsholt Down, Wantage OX12 9XD
T: 01367 820272 **M:** 07799 833115
E: pendomeffect@aol.com
1 £80 2 £70 (£45)
V DRY ★★
Some rooms en-suite
3 £5/person 1 £20
DRY
4 £15 8 £5
Down Barn is an organic farm. Evening meals not available every Sunday. Call in advance to arrange horsebox parking.

Star Inn INN

The Manager
Watery Lane, Sparsholt, Wantage OX12 9PL
T: 01235 751539
2 £65 4 £65 2 £85 (£55)
V VISA Most major cards. All rooms en-suite

Westcot Lodge *closed Xmas* B&B

Mrs P Upton
Westcot, Wantage OX12 9QA
T: 01235 751251 **M:** 07730 124888
E: philippaupton@hotmail.com
1 £75 1 £75 (£50) 1 £40
V DRY
Fee charged for transport to evening meal. Private bathroom available

Wayland's Smithy long barrow

Section 3

Sparsholt Firs to Streatley

This 17.4 miles (27.9km) stretch keeps to the high scarp edge before losing height towards the end as it drops into the Thames Valley. It includes the widest parts of the Trail and some of the best conditions underfoot. This is racehorse country with gallops alongside the Trail in many places.

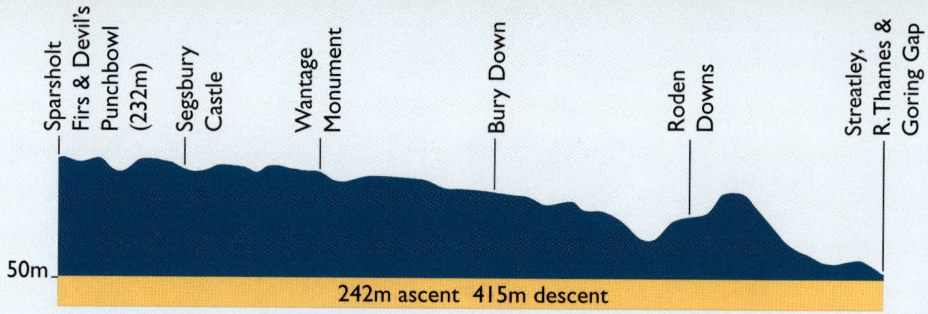

Maps

Landranger maps	174	Newbury and Wantage
Explorer maps	170	Abingdon, Wantage and Vale of White Horse

Taxis

Place	Name	Telephone Number
Childrey	Berkeley Executive Cars	07775 647790
East Challow	Grove Cabs	01235 772200
	Bonny's Taxis	07753 165890
Wantage	Cab Co	01235 772424
	Chapel Cars	07789 551931
	Evenlode Taxis	01235 762035
	Keith's of Wantage	01235 763344
	Stuart's Taxis	01235 770608
	Webb's of Wantage	07881 647777
East Ilsley	Ridgeway Travel	07780 686454
Aston Upthorpe	Astons Airport Services	07837 343680

Car Parking

If you choose to park in villages close to The Ridgeway, please park considerately. Other places to park are listed below but you need to be aware that theft from cars parked in the countryside does occur. You are advised to leave any unnecessary items at home or, failing that, ensure that anything valuable is locked in the boot of your vehicle.

Place	Map Grid Reference
On Ridgeway at Sparsholt Firs on the south side of B4001, 2½ miles (4km) south of Childrey	SU 344851
On Ridgeway on the east side of B4494, 3 miles (5km) south of Wantage	SU 417843
On Ridgeway at Scutchamer's Knob, 2 miles (3km) south of East Hendred off the A417 east of Wantage	SU 458851
On Ridgeway at Bury Down on minor road from A34 to West Ilsley (signed Ridgeway from A34)	SU 479841
On Ridgeway at end of Rectory Road, Streatley, west off A417	SU 567813

Water Points

* with troughs for animals

Place	Map Grid Reference
Hill Barn, Sparsholt Firs*	SU 338854
The Court Hill Ridgeway Centre (YHA), Letcombe Regis*	SU 393849
Compton Downs*	SU 506828

Toilets

Place	Map Grid Reference
The Court Hill Ridgeway Centre (YHA), Letcombe Regis	SU 393849

Vets

* large animal vets

Place	Name	Telephone Number
Lambourn	The Drove Veterinary Clinic	01488 71505
	Valley Equine Hospital*	01488 71999
Wantage	Abivale Veterinary Group	01235 770333
	Danetree Veterinary Surgeons	01235 770227
Cholsey	Larkmead Veterinary Group* - for equine	01491 651379 01491 651479
Goring-on-Thames	The Goring Veterinary Centre	01491 873638

Farriers

Place	Name	Telephone Number
Wantage	GP Feltham	07768 637068
	RGD Godfrey	01235 868492
Blewbury	Ian Belcher	01235 850029

After harvest near Streatley

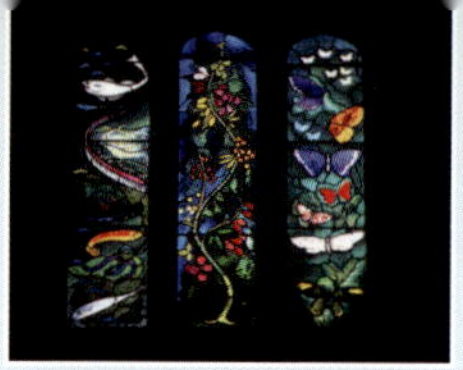

Saddlers

Place	Name	Telephone Number
Challow Station	Horse Shoe Saddlery	01367 710797
Childrey	White Horse Animal Feeds (no tack)	01235 751529
Denchworth	Denchworth Equestrian Supplies	01235 886175
Blewbury	Total Equestrian	01189 714554

Riding Stables for Guided Riding

Place	Name	Telephone Number
Kingston Lisle	Holistic Horses	01367 820033
Blewbury	Blewbury Riding & Training Centre	01235 851016

Horsebox Parking

The following places have sufficient space for you to park your horsebox. You **must** call in advance to arrange as space may be scarce. A fee may also be charged.

Place	Name	Telephone Number
Sparsholt Firs	Hill Barn (Accommodation guests and day-riders)	01235 751236
Lockinge	Lockinge Kiln Farm (Accommodation guests and day-riders - donation to Riding for the Disabled)	01235 763308

Bike Repairs

Place	Name	Telephone Number
Wantage	Ridgeway Cycles	01235 764445
	GMC	01235 764204
Abingdon	Behind Bars Cycle Shop	01235 533287
	Pedal Power	01235 525123
Didcot	Mountain Mania	01235 759366
Goring-on-Thames	Mountain Mania	01491 871721

Mountain Bike Hire

Place	Name	Telephone Number
Abingdon	Behind Bars	01235 533287
Goring-on-Thames	Mountain Mania	01491 871721

Tourist Information Centres

These TICs are staffed but note that many libraries in the area have leaflets about local attractions and events.

★ offers accommodation booking service

Place	Address/Opening Hours
★ Wantage	Vale and Downland Museum & Visitor Centre 19 Church Street, Wantage OX12 8BL **T**: 01235 771447 **E**: tourism@wantage-museum.com Opening hours: All year: Mon-Sat 10:00-16:00
Abingdon	Visitor Information Centre, Old Abbey House, Abbey Close, Abingdon OX14 3JD **T**: 01235 522711 www.abingdon.gov.uk Opening hours: Mon-Fri 9:00-17:00 (closed Bank Holidays) Sat 10:00-15:00 (Oct-May) Sat 10:00-16:00 (June Sep)

John Piper window in Farnborough church

Letcombe Regis

SU3886 1.2 miles (0.7km)
Didcot 10 miles (16km)

S M T W T F S

Pub: Greyhound Inn 01235 771093 - pub for sale as Companion went to print, so check for opening times

Brook Barn — B&B

Mr Mark Ashman
Letcombe Regis, Wantage OX12 9JD
T: 01235 766502
E: info@brookbarn.com
www.brookbarn.com
5 £90 1 £90 (£60) V DRY Most major cards. All rooms en-suite ★★★★★
VisitBritain Gold Award. Evening meals Friday to Sunday only

9 Croft End — B&B

Mrs Joyce Coombs
Letcombe Regis, Wantage OX12 9JJ
T: 01235 763694 **M:** 07762 566575
E: joyce.coombs@dsl.pipex.com
2 £65 1 £65 (£40) V DRY Some rooms en-suite
Lift provided for evening meal when not available locally

Court Hill Centre

The Manager
Court Hill, Letcombe Regis, Wantage OX12 9NE
T: 01235 760253
E: info@courthill.org.uk
www.courthill.org.uk
V DRY Most major cards.
Several £7/person DRY
Dormitory and small family rooms available from £18/person. Dogs on leads at all times on campsite

B&B **Quince Cottage**

Mrs Louise Boden
Letcombe Regis, Wantage OX12 9JP
T: 01235 763652 **M:** 07853 906813
E: louise.boden@bodenfamily.info
www.bodenfamily.info
1 £75 (£40) 2 £30 V
DRY
Private bathroom available. 3rd bed in twin £15 extra. Lift provided for evening meal when not available locally

Wantage

SU4088 2.5 miles (4km)
Didcot 8 miles (13km)

Town with full range of services, visit www.wantage.com for further details. It has a wide range of accommodation - details from Visitor Centre (see section introduction). Farmers Market last Saturday of each month.

☆ The Vale & Downland Museum
T: 01235 771447
www.wantage-museum.com.

Blackthorn

Locking e

SU4287 2.1 miles (3.4km)
Didcot 7.5 miles (12km)

Lockinge Kiln Farm *closed Dec-March* B&B

SU424834 0.6miles(1km) south of Ridgeway
Mrs Stella Cowan
Chain Hill, Wantage OX12 8PA
T: 01235 763308
E: cowan.stella@yahoo.com
www.lockingekiln.co.uk
1 £70 1 £65 (£38) (min age 10) V DRY One room en-suite, one private shower
2 £12 6 £10
Free lift to Wantage for evening meal but guests pay for taxi back. Horsebox parking for guests and day raiders - donation to riding for the disabled

Ardington

SU4388 2.5 miles (4km)
Didcot 6 miles (10km)

S M T W T F S
S M T W T F S
S M T W T F S
S M T W T F S
S M T W T F S

in shop
Pub: Boar's Head 01235 833254

☆ Ardington House (open summer only) **T:** 01235 821566

Boar's Head

Mr Bruce Buchan
Church Street, Ardington, Wantage OX12 8QA
T: 01235 833254
E: info@boarsheadardington.co.uk
www.boarsheadardington.co.uk
3 £95 (£80) V
All major credit cards.
★★★★ All rooms en-suite
No evening meal on Sundays. Free WiFi

Farnborough

SU4382 1.8 miles (2.9km)
Newbury 11.3 miles (18km)

☆ John Betjeman memorial window by John Piper in church

B&B
Old Smithy

Mrs Lorna Gwinner
Farnborough, Wantage OX12 8NX
T: 01488 638782 **M:** 07702 095371
E: info@oldsmithybandb.co.uk
www.oldsmithybandb.co.uk
2 £65 1 £65 (£45) (min age 12)
Transport available to pub for evening meal. Complimentary tea and cakes on arrival

West Hendred

SU4488 2.5 miles (4km)
Didcot 6 miles (9km)

S M T W T F S   S M T W T F S

Pub: Hare 01235 833249

East Hendred

SU4688 2.5 miles (4km)
Didcot 4 miles (7km)

S M T W T F S   S M T W T F S
S M T W T F S   S M T W T F S

☆ Hendred Museum: April-Oct Sundays 14:30-16:30. Nov-Easter 1st Sunday of month 14:30-15:30
T: 01235 835092
www.hendredmuseum.org.uk

☆ Hendred Vineyard
www.hendredvineyard.co.uk

B&B Cowdrays *closed Xmas & Easter*

Mr and Mrs John Bateman
Cat Street, East Hendred, Wantage
OX12 8JT
T: 01235 833313 **M:** 07799 622003
E: enquiries@cowdrays.co.uk
www.cowdrays.co.uk
2 £80 1 £70 (£35) 1 £35
V DRY
Some rooms en-suite ★★★

B&B Monk's Court

Mrs Susie Turnbull
Newbury Road, East Hendred, Wantage
OX12 8LG
T: 01235 833797 **M:** 07710 274653
E: susieturnbull@monkscourt.co.uk
www.monkscourt.co.uk
2 £70 1 £70 (£40) V
DRY ★★★
Some rooms en-suite

Greensands Guest House B&B

Ms Debbie Cox
Reading Road, East Hendred, Wantage
OX12 8JE
T: 01235 833338
E: greensands@btconnect.com
www.greensandsbandb.co.uk
4 £70 4 £70 (£50) 4 £85
V DRY
Mastercard, Visa. All rooms en-suite

West Ilsley

SU4782 1.2 miles (2km)
Didcot 7 miles (11km)

S M T W T F S   S M T W T F S

Pub: Harrow Inn 01635 281260

Chilton

SU4986 1.2 miles (2km)
Didcot 4 miles (6km) PF

S M T W T F S   S M T W T F S
S M T W T F S

Pub: Rose & Crown 01235 862992

East Ilsley

SU4981 1.2 miles (2km)
Didcot 7 miles (11km)

S M T W T F S   S M T W T F S

Pubs: Crown and Horns 01635 281545
Swan Hotel 01635 281238

Crown & Horns Inn

Mr Steve Collins
Compton Road, East Ilsley RG20 7LH
T: 01635 281545
E: stevecllns948@gmail.com
www.crownandhorns.co.uk
4 £55 2 £60 1 £65 V DRY Most major cards. All rooms en-suite

Swan Hotel *closed 24-26 Dec*

Mr Richard Vellender
High St, East Ilsley RG20 7LF
T: 01635 281238
E: kimrichstar@aol.com
www.theswaneastilsley.co.uk
2 £75 3 £69 (£69) (min age 12) V DRY Most major cards. All rooms en-suite
Evening meals not available Sundays. Multiple night breaks available, see advert opposite

Upton

SU5186 2.5 miles (4km)
Didcot 3 miles (5km)

S M T W T F S   S M T W T F S

Pub: George & Dragon 01235 850723
Food served only to 7pm Sunday

Prospect House *closed Xmas* B&B

Mrs Hilary Powell
Upton, Didcot OX11 9HU
T: 01235 850268 **M:** 07966 205688
E: hilary_powell@btinternet.com
www.prospect-house.info
1 £70 1 £70 (£40) 1 £80 V DRY ★★★
2 £15 4 £5
Free parking for guests' horseboxes up to 7.5 tons

Hogweed

Compton

SU5280 1.2 miles (2km)
Goring 6 miles (9km) PF

S M T W T F S   S M T W T F S

S M T W T F S   S M T W T F S

Pubs: Compton Swan 01635 579400

Compton Swan — *closed 1 Jan*

Jean-Marc Bidegain & Penelope Sexton
High Street, Compton, Newbury
RG20 6NJ
T: 01635 579400 **M:** 07970 484642
E: comptonswan@googlemail.com
www.comptonswan.co.uk
6 £85 V DRY Most major cards
★★★★ All rooms en-suite
Evening meal on Sundays only by prior arrangement

Blewbury

SU5385 2.5 miles (4km)
Didcot 4 miles (6km) PF

S M T W T F S   S M T W T F S

S M T W T F S

Barley Mow

Owen and Josephine O'Reilly
London Road, Blewbury OX11 9NU
T: 01235 850296
1 £70 1 £75 1 £85 1 £40 V ★★★ All rooms en-suite
No evening meals Sunday to Tuesday

Blewbury Centre

Jane Dexter
Bessels Way, Blewbury OX11 9NH
T: 01235 851016
E: info@blewburycentre.co.uk
www.blewburycentre.co.uk
20 £5
Café open Saturdays and competition days 10am-4pm. For group bookings extended café facilities by arrangement

Dragonwyke — B&B

Mrs Sharon Pegram
South Street, Blewbury OX11 9PR
T: 01235 850412 **M:** 07791 799925
E: dragonwyke@scpegram.demon.co.uk
www.smoothhound.co.uk/hotels/dragonwyke.html
1 £70 (£50) 1 £85 1 £35 V DRY Some rooms en-suite

Red Lion

INN

Matt Wardle and Kerry Tombs
Chapel Lane, Blewbury OX11 9PQ
T: 01235 850403
E: enquiries@redlionblewbury.co.uk
www.redlionblewbury.co.uk
1 £75 (£65) V DRY All major cards. Room is en-suite
No evening meal Sundays. Free WiFi

Yew Tree

B&B

Mrs Liz Thacker
London Road, Blewbury OX11 9PF
T: 01235 850678
E: lizthackeryewtree@hotmail.com
www.smoothhound.co.uk/a54126.html
1 £65 (£50) 1 £40 (min age 12) V DRY One room en-suite
WiFi internet access available

ASTON UPTHORPE

SU5986 3.3 miles (5.3km)
Didcot 3.7 miles (5.9km)

S M T W T F S   S M T W T F S

Pub/restaurant: Sweet Olive 01235 851272 (closed Feb and two weeks in July)

Middle Fell

B&B

Mrs Christine Millin
Moreton Road, Aston Upthorpe, Didcot OX11 9ER
T: 01235 850207 **M:** 07833 920678
E: middlefell@ic24.net
www.middlefell.co.uk
1 £75 1 £55 (£38) 1 £115 1 £38 V DRY
★★★★ All rooms en-suite

ALDWORTH

SU5579 1.2 miles (2km)
Goring 3 miles (5km)

S M T W T F S   S M T W T F S

S M T W T F S   S M T W T F S

Pubs: Bell 01635 578272 & Four Points 01635 578367
www.aldworth.info

Fieldview Cottage *closed Xmas*

B&B

Mrs Bette Hunt
Bell Lane, Aldworth, Reading RG8 9SB
T: 01635 578964 **M:** 07765 832764
E: haroldhunt@btinternet.com
1 £70 1 £70 1 £35 V DRY ★★★★
All rooms have private bathrooms. Lift available to pub for evening meal

Moulsford

SU5983 1.2 miles (2km)
Cholsey 2 miles (3km)

S M T W T F S   S M T W T F S

Pub: Beetle & Wedge 01491 651381

B&B

Beetle & Wedge Boathouse
closed 1st week Jan

Mrs Stephanie Musk
Ferry Lane, Moulsford OX10 9JF
T: 01491 651381
E: boathouse@beetleandwedge.co.uk
www. beetleandwedge.co.uk
/ 3 £90 (£75) V
DRY All major cards.
★★★★ All rooms en-suite

Streatley

SU5980 on path
Goring & Streatley 0.5 miles (1km)

S M T W T F S   S M T W T F S

Pubs: Swan at Streatley 01491 878800 & Bull 01491 872392

☆ The Holies Nature Reserve
T: 0118 984 3040
www.nationaltrust.org.uk

☆ Basildon Park
T: 0118 984 3040
www.nationaltrust.org.uk

☆ Beale Wildlife Park
T: 0844 826 1761 www.bealepark.co.uk

Swan at Streatley

The Manager
Streatley RG8 9HR
T: 01491 878800
E: sales@swan-at-streatley.co.uk
www.swanatstreatley.co.uk
25 £125 8 £125 2 £155 (£115) 9 £105 V
All major cards ★★★★ All rooms en-suite
Free WiFi

Bull at Streatley

The Manager
Reading Road, Streatley RG8 9JJ
T: 01491 872392
E: bullatstreatley@hotmail.co.uk
www.thebullatstreatley.com
6 £75 1 £100 V
All major cards. All rooms en-suite

YHA Streatley

Mr Nick Crivich
Hill House, Reading Road, Streatley RG8 9JJ
T: 01491 872278
E: streatley@yha.org.uk
www.yha.org.uk
2 £38 8 £40 (min age 2)
V DRY Most major cards ★★★
Self-catering accommodation from £10/night. WiFi available

B&B **3 Icknield Cottages**

Mrs Susan Brodie
High Street, Streatley RG8 9JA
T: 01491 875152 **M:** 07989 152295
E: mikeandsuebrodie@btinternet.com
1 £30 V DRY
Private bathroom

SC **Linden Cottage**

Mrs Sue Jubb
Streatley RG8 9NB
T: 01491 871120 **M:** 07747 388957
E: sue_jubb@hotmail.com
www.lindencottages.co.uk
Self-catering, accessible cottage, sleeps 4 from £250/week.

Linksdown Studio B&B SC

Mrs Gaye Walsh
Rectory Road, Streatley RG8 9QA
T: 01491 873139 **M:** 07855 600985
E: gayewalsh@googlemail.com
www.linksdownbedandbreakfast.co.uk
1 £70 V DRY Room is en-suite
2 £5
Self-catering £65/night

Stable Cottages B&B

Mrs Diana Fenton
Wallingford Road, Streatley RG8 9JX
T: 01491 874408
1 £60 (£30) 1 £30 (min age 8) V DRY
2 £15
Horsebox parking nearby

Roden Downs, north of Compton

Brunel's Bridge, north of South Stoke

Grim's Ditch east of Wallingford during Spring

Section 4

Streatley to Watlington

At the start of this 15.3 miles (24.6km) section The Ridgeway crosses another National Trail, the Thames Path, before following the bank of the River Thames for a few picturesque miles. The Trail then heads east into the more wooded Chilterns via an ancient Grim's Ditch and finishes on the wide track of the old Icknield Way.

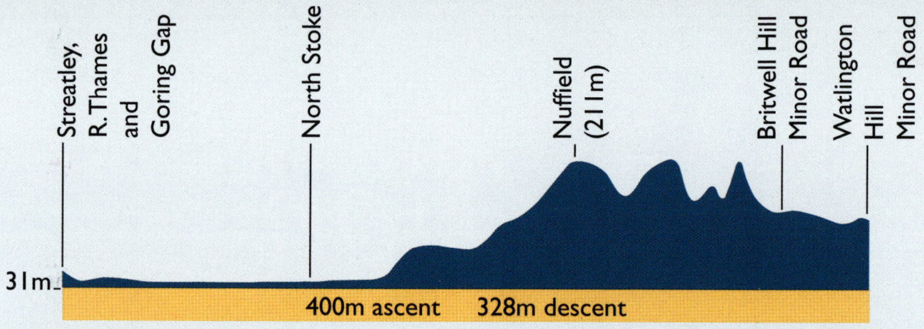

Maps

Landranger maps	174	Newbury and Wantage
	175	Reading and Windsor
Explorer maps	171	Chiltern Hills West

Taxis

Place	Name	Telephone Number
Goring-on-Thames	Airpal Taxis	07862 721698
Wallingford	Hills Taxis	01491 837022
Nettlebed	David Byers of Nettlebed	01491 641159

Car Parking

If you choose to park in villages close to The Ridgeway, please park considerately. Other places to park are listed below but you need to be aware that theft from cars parked in the countryside does occur. You are advised to leave any unnecessary items at home or, failing that, ensure that anything valuable is locked in the boot of your vehicle.

Place	Map Grid Reference
Goring-on-Thames public car park	SU 599807
On Ridgeway on west side of minor road, 1 mile (1½km) from Britwell Salome heading southeast	SU 681922
On Ridgeway on east side of Hill Road, minor road to Christmas Common ½ mile (1km) southeast of Watlington	SU 698940

Water Points

Place	Map Grid Reference
Grimsdyke Cottage, Grim's Ditch	SU 660872
Church, Nuffield (on the wall)	SU 667874
White Mark Farm Camp Site, Watlington (March - Nov)	SU 697939

Toilets

Place	Map Grid Reference
Goring-on-Thames (Car Park off Station Road)	SU 602807
White Mark Farm Camp Site, Watlington (March - October)	SU 697939
Watlington (High Street) ♿	SU 689945

Vets

* large animal vets

Place	Name	Telephone Number
Goring-on-Thames	The Goring Veterinary Centre	01491 873638
Cholsey	Larkmead Veterinary Group* - for equine	01491 651379 01491 651479
Wallingford	Abivale Veterinary Group	01491 839043
Watlington	Crossroads Veterinary Centre	01491 612799

Farriers

Place	Name	Telephone Number
Watlington	Adrian Spilsbury	07968 065991

Saddlers

Place	Name	Telephone Number
Blewbury	Total Equestrian	01189 714554

Horsebox Parking

The following places have sufficient space for you to park your horsebox. You **must** call in advance to arrange as space may be scarce. A fee may also be charged.

Place	Name	Telephone Number
Ewelme	Mays Farms (Accommodation guests and day-riders)	01491 642056

Bike Repairs

Place	Name	Telephone Number
Goring-on-Thames	Mountain Mania	01491 871721
Wallingford	Rides on Air	01491 836289
Thame	2 Wheels	01844 212455
	Thame Cycles	01844 261520

Mountain Bike Hire

Place	Name	Telephone Number
Goring-on-Thames	Mountain Mania	01491 871721
Thame	Helpful Hirings	01844 212468

Visitor Information Centres

This VIC is staffed but note that many libraries in the area also have leaflets about local attractions and events.

Place	Address/Opening Hours
Wallingford	Wallingford Town Information Centre, Town Hall, Market Place, Wallingford OX10 0EG **T**: 01491 826972 www.wallingford.co.uk Opening hours: Mar to mid Dec: Mon to Fri 10:00-16:00 (closed 12:30-13:00) Sat 10:00-14:00 Mid-Dec to Feb: Mon to Sat 10:00-14:00 (closed Bank Hols)

View over Goring-on-Thames

Goring-on-Thames

SU6080 **on path**
Goring & Streatley P£
WC

	S	M	T	W	T	F	S

£ HSBC, Lloyds TSB
www.goring-on-thames.co.uk

INN **John Barleycorn**

Mr & Mrs Hurst
Manor Road, Goring-on-Thames
RG8 9DP
T: 01491 872509 **E:** johnbarleycorn-goring@btconnect.com
www.thejohnbarleycornpub.co.uk
3 £75 (min age 12) V Most major cards. All rooms en-suite
No evening meals on Sundays

B&B **Melrose Cottage**

Mrs Rosemary Howarth
36 Milldown Road, Goring-on-Thames
RG8 0BD
T: 01491 873040 **M:** 07798 663897
E: melrose-cottage@goring-on-thames.co.uk
2 £60 (£40) 1 £35 V DRY
Free WiFi, fridge in room

Miller of Mansfield H

William Green
High Street, Goring-on-Thames RG8 9AW
T: 01491 872829
E: reservations@millerofmansfield.com
www.millerofmansfield.com
12 £110 1 £130 (£70) 2 £180 V All major cards. All rooms en-suite
Free WiFi

Queens Arms INN

Mr Chris Wilson
Reading Road, Goring-on-Thames
RG8 0ER
T: 01491 872825
2 £30 3 £30 V DRY All major cards.
Free WiFi

Southview House B&B

Mr and Mrs Dawn and Richard Roberts
Farm Road, Goring-on-Thames RG8 0AA
T: 01491 872184 **M:** 07957 571620
E: goringbnb@rglroberts.com
/ 3 £70 (£55) V DRY 2 private bathrooms
Free WiFi

South Stoke

SU5983 on path
Goring & Streatley 2 miles (3km)

S M T W T F S   S M T W T F S

Pub: Perch & Pike 01491 872415

Perch & Pike (INN)

Mr Neil Dorsett
The Street, South Stoke, Reading RG8 0JS
T: 01491 872415
E: info@perchandpike.co.uk
www.perchandpike.co.uk
3 £85 1 £85 V All major cards. ★★★ All rooms en-suite.

No evening meals on Sundays unless by arrangement. Cycle storage not entirely secure.

Oak Barn (B&B)

Mrs Vanessa Guiver
The Old Post Office, The Street, South Stoke, Reading RG8 0JS
T: 01491 871872 **M:** 07889 757767
E: vanessa.guiver@btinternet.com
www.oakbarn.org
1 £80 V DRY Room is en-suite

Internet available

North Stoke

SU6086 on path
Goring & Streatley 4 miles (6km)

S M T W T F S   S M T W T F S

Pub: Springs Hotel 01491 836687

Briar Cottage (B&B)

Mrs Zazie Carruthers
1 The Street, North Stoke, Wallingford OX10 6BL
T: 01491 835833 **M:** 07969 462844
E: richardzazie@btinternet.com
1 £65 (£40) V DRY Room is en-suite

Springs Hotel (H)

Miss Karen Spiers
1 Wallingford Road, North Stoke, Wallingford OX10 6BE
T: 01491 836687
E: reception@thespringshotel.com
www.thespringshotel.com
29 £105 3 £105 (£90) V Most major cards. All rooms en-suite

CROWMARSH GIFFORD

SU6189 0.6 miles (1km)
Didcot 6 miles (10km)

S M T W T F S S M T W T F S

S M T W T F S S M T W T F S

Pubs: Queen's Head 01491 839857 & Bell Inn (Hungry Horse) 01491 835324

☆ Riverside Park & Swimming Pool
T: 01491 835232

B&B **Little Gables**

Mr Paul Reeves
166 Crowmarsh Hill, Wallingford
OX10 8BG
T: 01491 837834
E: mail@littlegables.co.uk
www.littlegables.co.uk
1 £75 1 £75 1 £100 1 £60 V DRY All major cards ★★★★ All rooms en-suite

Bridge Villa Camping & Caravan Park *closed Jan*

Mr Andrew Townsend
The Street, Crowmarsh Gifford,
Wallingford OX10 8HB
T: 01491 836860 **M:** 07801 274116
E: eltownsendandson@btinternet.com
www.bridgevilla.co.uk
£9 £17 WC DRY CG Most major cards
110 pitches in total

Maran Cottage B&B

Mrs Christine Buckland-Jones
Old Reading Road, Crowmarsh Gifford,
Wallingford OX10 8EN
T: 01491 839122 **M:** 07952 865396
1 £50 (£40) V DRY Room is en-suite
Room can be family with cot/child bed £60

Riverside Park *closed mid-Oct - Easter*

The Manager
The Street, Wallingford Bridge,
Crowmarsh Gifford, Wallingford
OX10 8EB
T: 01491 835232 (out of season 01865 341035)
E: rachael.spindler@nexuscommunity.org
www.nexuscommunity.org
or 18 £12 WC

South Stoke church

4 Streatley to Watlington

WALLINGFORD

SU6089 1.2 miles (2km)
Cholsey 6 miles (9km)

Town with full range of services, visit www.wallingford.co.uk for further details. Farmers Market 3rd Tues and 5th Sat of the month. Local Producers Market most Sats

☆ Wallingford Museum
T: 01491 835065
www.wallingfordmuseum.org.uk

☆ Wallingford Castle
www.berkshirehistory.com/castles/wallingford_cast.html

George Hotel — *closed 1Jan*

Mr Oliver Round-Turner
High Street, Wallingford OX10 0BS
T: 01491 836665
E: rooms@george-hotel-wallingford.com
www.peelhotel.com
24 £115 4 £115 2 £140 (£110) 9 £98 V All major cards ★★★ All rooms en-suite
Free WiFi

Huntington House — *closed Xmas & New Year* — B&B

Mike and Julie Huntington
18 Wood Street Wallingford OX10 0AX
M: 07831 546047
E: hunting311@aol.com
www.huntington-house.co.uk
2 £65 (£50) 1 £50 V DRY ★★★
One double room converts to twin

52 Blackstone Road — B&B

Mrs Enid Barnard
Wallingford OX10 8JL
T: 01491 839339
E: enid.barnard@googlemail.com
1 £45 (£35) 1 £23 V DRY
Fee charged for lift to pubs

Old School House — *closed 22-28 Dec* — B&B

Mrs Carolyn Bristow
23 Castle Street Wallingford OX10 8DW
T: 01491 839571 **M:** 07900 225167
E: bristow.carolyn@gmail.com
www.23oldschoolhouse.com
2 £75 (£70) 1 £105 V DRY Some rooms en-suite

Hailey

SU6485 1.4 miles (2.3km)
Cholsey 5.3 miles (8.5km)

S M T W T F S S M T W T F S

Pub: King William IV 01491 681845

Nuffield

SU6687 on path
Henley-on-Thames 7 miles (11km)

S M T W T F S S M T W T F S

Pub: Crown Inn 01491 641335 www.brakspear.co.uk. Reopening 2012, check for opening times

B&B **14 Bradley Road** *closed Xmas & New Year*

Ms Diana Chambers
Nuffield, Henley-on-Thames RG9 5SG
T: 01491 641359 **M:** 07974 548528
E: dianamc@waitrose.com
1 £60 1 £60 V DRY One room en-suite
Small charge for lift to pub for evening meal

Mays Farm House B&B

SU654885 1.3 miles (2.1km) from Ridgeway
Mrs Sue Veitch
Ewelme, Wallingford OX10 6QF
T: 01491 642056 **M:** 07791 121405
E: sue@maysfarmewelme.co.uk
www.maysfarmewelme.co.uk
1 £55 (£40) 1 £35 V DRY
2 £5
Lift to pubs £3 each way. Free horsebox parking for guests and day-riders

Walkers in the Chilterns

4 Streatley to Watlington

Nettlebed

SU70787 2.9 miles (4.6km)
Henley-on-Thames 5.2 miles (8.4km) PF

Pub: White Hart Hotel 01491 641245

White Hart

The Manager
28 High Street, Nettlebed RG9 5DD
T: 01491 641245
E: info.hart@tmsteaks.co.uk
www.whitehartnettlebed.com
11 £70 1 £70 V All major cards ★★★★ All rooms en-suite
Free WiFi

B&B

Somerset

Mrs Nan McDonnell
9 High Street, Nettlebed, Henley-on-Thames RG9 5DA
T: 01491 641710 M: 07854 531499
E: jandnmcd@greenbee.net
2 £70 (£35) V DRY

Ewelme

SU6491 1.3 miles (2.1km)
Henley-on-Thames 10.6 miles (17km) PF

Pub: Shepherd's Hut 01491 835636

☆ Ewelme Watercress Beds. Open first Sunday of month. T: 01494 835173 www.ewelmewatercressbeds.org

Fords Farm

B&B SC

Miss Marlene Edwards
Ewelme, Wallingford OX10 6HU
T: 01491 839272 **E:** fordsfarm@callnetuk.com
www.fordsfarm.co.uk
1 £75 2 £75 (£50) (min age 10) V DRY Mastercard, Visa ★★★★★ Some rooms en-suite
VisitBritain Gold Award. Self-catering unit £165/night or £700/week

Park Corner

SU6988 1.2 miles (2km)
Henley-on-Thames 6 miles (10km)

Park Corner Farmhouse

B&B

Mrs Susan Rutter
Park Corner, Nettlebed, Henley-on-Thames RG9 6DX
T: 01491 641450 **E:** parkcorner_farmhouse@hotmail.com
2 £70 (£40) (min age 5) V
DRY
Free transport for evening meal

Watlington

SU6894 0.6 miles (1km)
Henley-on-Thames 10 miles (16km) PF WC
Small town with a range of services

☆ Watlington Hill and White Mark
www.nationaltrust.org.uk

Harebells

Fat Fox Inn

Mr John Riddell
13 Shirburn Street, Watlington OX49 5BU
T: 01491 613040 **M:** 07788 920108
E: info@thefatfoxinn.co.uk
www.thefatfoxinn.co.uk
5 £79 4 £79 (£69)
V All major cards. All rooms en-suite

Woodgate Orchard Cottage

B&B

Ms Ronnie Roper
Howe Road, Watlington OX49 5EL
T: 01491 612675
E: ronnie.m.roper@gmail.com
3 £70 1 £70 (£48) V
DRY
Charge for lift to/from Ridgeway

White Mark Farm *closed 30 Nov-1 Mar*

Mrs Debbie Bacon
82 Hill Road, Watlington OX49 5AF
T: 01491 612295
E: debbie.whitemarkfarm@yahoo.co.uk
www.whitemark.co.uk
50 £6/person 5 £6/person
DRY
Fridge, microwave and kettle available

The Chilterns Area of Outstanding Natural Beauty

Near Aston Rowant

Section 5

Watlington to Wendover

This 17 miles (27.2km) stretch is probably the most strenuous part of The Ridgeway. It starts out gently enough following the wide track of the Icknield Way but once it departs from this it climbs in and out of several Chilterns valleys. Passing through some lovely nature reserves the Trail reaches a high point with fantastic views at Coombe Hill before descending to Wendover. If you haven't already seen a red kite, you're guaranteed to see one on this stretch!

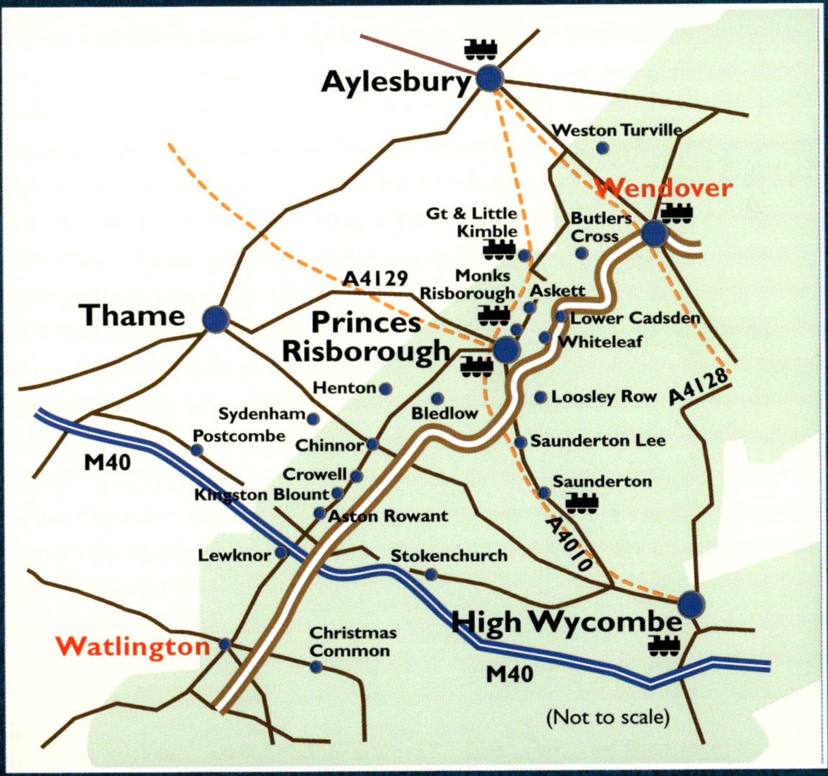

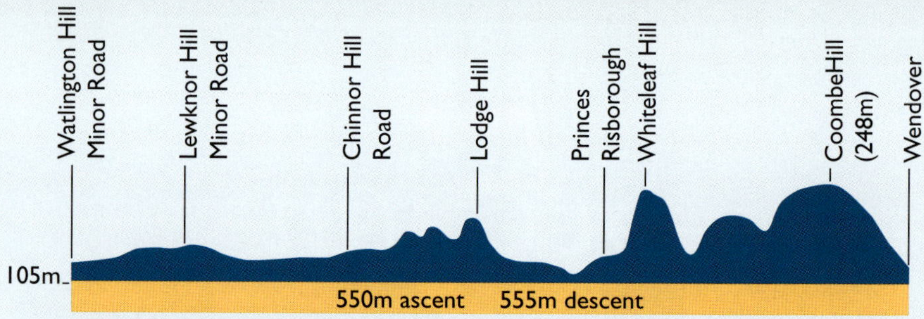

Maps

Landranger maps	175	Reading and Windsor
	165	Aylesbury and Leighton Buzzard
Explorer maps	171	Chiltern Hills West
	181	Chiltern Hills North

Taxis

Place	**Name**	**Telephone Number**
Chinnor	Chinnor Cabs	01844 353637
Loosley Row	Springline Cars	01844 274474
Princes Risborough	Risborough Cars	01844 274111
	Village Cars	01844 342551
	B&V Taxis	01844 342079
	Red Line Cars	01844 343736
Wendover	Alexander's	01296 620888

Car Parking

If you choose to park in villages close to The Ridgeway, please park considerately. Other places to park are listed below but you need to be aware that theft from cars parked in the countryside does occur. You are advised to leave any unnecessary items at home or, failing that, ensure that anything valuable is locked in the boot of your vehicle.

Place	**Map Grid Reference**
On Ridgeway on east side of minor road to Bledlow Ridge ½ mile (1km) south of Chinnor	SP 761003
Princes Risborough public car park	SP 810034
Whiteleaf car park, ½ mile (1km) east of Princes Risborough. Turn right off A4010 at Monks Risborough and car park is on left at top of escarpment	SP 824036
National Trust car park for Coombe Hill, 1 mile (2km) southwest of Wendover. From Wendover travel west on minor road to Princes Risborough. Take first left, then first left again. At top of hill car park is on left	SP 852062
Wendover public car park	SP 868077

Water Points

Place	Map Grid Reference
White Mark Farm Camp Site, Watlington (March - October)	SU 697939
Aston Rowant National Nature Reserve (close to A40 Ridgeway crossing)	SU 727976

Toilets

Place	Map Grid Reference
Watlington (High Street)	SU 689945
White Mark Farm Camp Site, Watlington (March- October)	SU 697939
Chinnor Village Centre (High Street)	SP 757012
Princes Risborough (Horn Mill Car Park)	SP 809033
Wendover (Library Car Park)	SP 868078

Vets

Place	Name	Telephone Number
Watlington	Crossroads Veterinary Centre	01491 612799
Stokenchurch	Hall Place Veterinary Centre	01494 485855
Princes Risborough	Sprinz & Nash	01844 345655
Halton	Wendover Heights Veterinary Centre	01296 623439

Farriers

Place	Name	Telephone Number
Watlington	Adrian Spilsbury	07968 065991
Chinnor	DM Goth	07734 113045
	N Kilner	07867 521476
Stokenchurch	John Jennings	07836 562784

Saddler

Place	Name	Telephone Number
Lacey Green	Widmer Feeds (no tack)	01844 344765
Speen, P Risborough	Beryl P Forrest	01494 488130

Horsebox Parking

The following places have sufficient space for you to park your horsebox. You **must** call in advance to arrange as space may be scarce. A fee may also be charged.

Place	Name	Telephone Number
Princes Risborough	Brimmers Farms (Campers and day-riders)	01844 346171

Bike Repairs

Place	Name	Telephone Number
Thame	Thame Cycles	01844 261520
Princes Risborough	Risborough Cycles	01844 345949/ 07739 614579
	Bicycle Workshop	07973 530914

Mountain Bike Hire

Place	Name	Telephone Number
Princes Risborough	Risborough Cycles	01844 345949
Tring	Mountain Mania	01442 822458

Visitor Information Centres

★ offers accommodation booking service (until 15:30)

Place	Address/Opening Hours
Wallingford	Town Hall, Market Place, Wallingford OX10 0EG **T**: 01491 826972 www.wallingford.co.uk Opening hours: Mar to mid Dec: Mon to Fri 10:00-16:00 (closed 12:30-13:00) Sat 10:00-14:00 Mid-Dec to Feb: Mon to Sat 10:00-14:00 (closed Bank Hols)
Princes Risborough	Tower Court, Horns Lane, Princes Risborough HP27 0AJ **T**: 01844 274795 www.visitbuckinghamshire.org **E**: risborough_office@wycombe.gov.uk Opening hours: All year: Mon-Wed, Fri 9:00-17:00; Thurs 10:00-17:00; Fri 9:00-17:00; Sat 9:00-13:00
★Wendover	The Clock Tower, High Street, Wendover HP22 6DU **T**: 01296 696759 www.wendover-pc.gov.uk Opening hours: All year: Mon-Sat 10:00-16:00

Christmas Common

SU7193 1.3 miles (2.1km)
Henley-on-Thames 9.6 miles (15.4km)

S M T W T F S   S M T W T F S

Pub: Fox & Hounds 01491 612599

Lewknor

SU7197 0.6 miles (1km)
Princes Risborough 7 miles (12km)

S M T W T F S   S M T W T F S

Pub: Leathern Bottle 01844 351482

B&B **Moorcourt Cottage** *Closed mid Dec to mid Mar*

Mrs Eppy Hodgson
Weston Road, Lewknor OX49 5RU
T: 01844 351419
E: moorcourt2002@yahoo.co.uk
1 £70 1 £70 (£45) V
DRY ★★★★ All rooms en-suite

Spindle

Postcombe

SU7099 1.6 miles (2.5km)
Princes Risborough 8 miles (13km)

S M T W T F S   S M T W T F S

S M T W T F S

Pub: England's Rose 01844 281383

England's Rose *Closed 25&26 Dec*

Ms Sheila Guinnane
London Road, Postcombe, Thame OX9 7DP
T: 01844 281383
E: info@englandsrosepub.co.uk
www.englandsrosepub.co.uk
2 £65 2 £65 1 £90
2 £40 V DRY
Most major cards. All rooms en-suite
Charge made for laundry

Aston Rowant

SU7298 0.6 miles (1km)
Princes Risborough 6 miles (10km)

S M T W T F S   S M T W T F S

Pub: Lambert Arms 01844 351496

☆ Aston Rowant National Nature Reserve
T: 01844 351833
www.naturalengland.org.uk

Lambert Arms

INN

Mr Andrew Edwards
London Road, Aston Rowant OX49 5SB
T: 01844 351496
E: info.lambertarms@bespokehotels.com
www.bespokehotels.com/hotel/pages/lambertarms/home.htm
31 £89 7 £89 1 £99 V Most major cards. ★★★★ All rooms en-suite
£10 charge for dogs. Free WiFi

Tower Cottage *closed Xmas & New Year*

B&B

Mrs Margaret Mason
Chinnor Road, Aston Rowant
OX49 5SH
T: 01844 354676
E: towercottagebb@aol.com
www.tower-cottage.co.uk
1 £55 2 £50 (£40) (min age 4) V DRY Some rooms en-suite

Stokenchurch

SU7696 2.7 miles (4.3km)
Princes Risborough or High Wycombe 7.3 miles (11.7km)

£ Lloyds TSB & three in local stores

Hallbottom Farm

B&B

Mrs Deborah Abbot
Park Lane, Stokenchurch HP14 3TQ
T: 01494 482520 **M:** 07778 216024
E: deborah@hallbottomfarm.co.uk
www.hallbottomfarm.co.uk
4 £80 2 £80 (£45) 1 £120 V DRY Some rooms en-suite
Charge for lift to/from Ridegway. Free transport to evening meal

Kingston Blount

SU7399 0.5 miles (0.8km)
Princes Risborough 6 miles (10km)

Pub: Cherry Tree 01844 352273

Lakeside Town Farm

B&B
SC

Mrs Theresa Clark
Town Farm Cottage, Brook Street, Kingston Blount OX39 4RZ
T: 01844 352152 **M:** 07971 436504
E: theresa@townfarmcottage.co.uk
www.townfarmcottage.co.uk
2 £85 1 £85 (£60) (min age 8) V DRY Most major cards ★★★★ All rooms en-suite
Self-catering facilities £100 per night

Cherry Tree

Mr Robert Wheatley
High Street, Kingston Blount OX39 4SJ
T: 01844 352273
E: info.thecherrytree@googlemail.com
www.thecherrytreepub.com
3 £50 1 £50 V
Most major cards
★★★ All rooms en-suite
No evening meals Sundays. Free WiFi

Crowell

SU7499 0.5 miles (0.8km)
Princes Risborough 5.6 miles (9km)

S M T W T F S   S M T W T F S

Pub: Shepherd's Crook 01844 351431

Chinnor

SP7500 0.6 miles (1km)
Princes Risborough 4 miles (7km) P F WC (closed Sat afternoon and Sunday)
Large village with range of services

☆ Chinnor Hill Nature Reserve
T: 01865 775476 www.bbowt.org.uk

☆ Chinnor and Princes Risborough Railway
T: 01844 353535 www.cprra.co.uk

Croft

closed Nov-April B&B

Mrs Beth Smith
Chinnor Hill, Chinnor OX39 4BS
T: 01844 353654 **M:** 07941 697873
E: bethsmith1@gmail.co.uk
www.bethatthecroft.co.uk
2 £60 (£55) DRY
★★★★ One room en-suite

Sydenham

SP7301 2.2 miles (3.6km)
Haddenham & Thame Parkway 6.1 miles (9.8km)

S M T W T F S   S M T W T F S

Pub: Crown Inn 01844 351634 & Inn at Emmington 01844 351367

Inn at Emmington

Mr Jerry Pattison
Sydenham Road, Sydenham, Chinnor OX39 4LD
T: 01844 351367
7 £79 1 £89 (£70) 1 £89
V Most major cards. All rooms en-suite
Charge for 3rd person in family room. No evening meal Sundays

Henton

SP7602 1 miles (1.5km)
Princes Risborough 3 miles (5km)

S M T W T F S   S M T W T F S

Pub: Peacock 01844 353519

B&B **Manor Farm Cottage**

Mr & Mrs Trevor & Jean Dixon
Henton, Chinnor OX39 4AE
T: 01844 353301 **M:** 07889 441601
E: dixonhenton@aol.com
www.manorfarmcottage.info
1 £60 (£45) 1 £80
V DRY
★★★★ One room en-suite, one private bathroom
VisitBritain Silver Award

Peacock *closed Xmas Day*

Mr Martin Roberts
Henton, Chinnor OX39 4AH
T: 01844 353519
E: escape@peacockcountryinn.co.uk
www.peacockcountryinn.co.uk
25 £120 7 £120 (£110) 1 £130 V
Most major cards. All rooms en-suite
Free WiFi

Bledlow

SP7702 0.6 miles (1km)
Princes Risborough 2 miles (3km)

S M T W T F S   S M T W T F S

Pub: Lions of Bledlow 01844 343345

☆ Lyde Gardens (next to church) open daily dawn to dusk.

Saunderton Lee

SP7901 0.6 miles (1km)
Saunderton 1.2 miles (2km)

S M T W T F S   S M T W T F S

Pub: Rose & Crown 01844 345299

Rose & Crown

Jonathan Levene
Wycombe Road, Saunderton, Princes Risborough HP27 9NP
T: 01844 345299
E: info@rosecrowninn.co.uk
www. rosecrowninn.co.uk
11 £70 1 £80 1 £80 2 £60 V DRY
All major cards. All rooms en-suite
No evening meal Sundays. Free WiFi

Loosley Row

SP8100 1.1 miles (1.7km)
Saunderton 2.4 miles (3.8km)

B&B SC

Greenhills Garden Apartment

Mrs D O Dean
Greenhills, Little Lane, Loosley Row, Princes Risborough HP27 0NX
T: 01844 342409
E: d.dean409@btinternet.com
www.princesrisborough-breakfast.co.uk
1 £75 DRY Most major cards. Room is en-suite
Apartment accommodation for max 4 people, can be self-catering with complimentary continental breakfast. £75 for 2 people and £20/additional person

Princes Risborough

SP8003 on path
Princes Risborough

Town with full range of services, visit www.visitbuckinghamshire.org for further details. Farmers Market 3rd Thurs of each month.

Brimmers Farm

SP820026 0.6 miles (1km) from Ridgeway
Mrs Sarah Uhart
Brimmers Road, Princes Risborough HP27 0LE
T: 01844 346171 **M:** 07951 485436
E: camping@brimmersfarm.co.uk
www.brimmersfarm.co.uk
10 £6/person DRY
4 £7
Horsebox parking for guests and day-riders £10/day

Ridgeway Lodge *closed Dec - end Feb*

B&B

Mrs Miv Hughes
Upper Icknield Way, Saunderton, Princes Risborough HP27 9NL
T: 01844 345438 **M:** 07828 078848
E: miv@ridgewaylodge.co.uk
www.ridgewaylodge.co.uk
2 £70 2 £78 (£45) V DRY Some rooms en-suite.
Ready meal provided if ordered in advance

Whiteleaf

SP8204 0.6 miles (1km)
Monks Risborough 1 miles (1.5km)

S M T W T F S S M T W T F S

Pub: Red Lion 01844 344476. Pub closes at 9pm on Mondays and 7pm during winter months on Sundays

☆ Whiteleaf Hill and Cross

Red Lion

Anthony Hibbert
Upper Icknield Way, Whiteleaf, Princes Risborough HP27 0LL
T: 01844 344476 **M:** 07881 777240
E: tim_hibbert@hotmail.com
www.theredlionwhiteleaf.co.uk
2 £60 2 £60 V Most major cards. All rooms en-suite
No evening meal Sundays and Mondays. Free WiFi

Lower Cadsden

SP8204 on path
Monks Risborough 1 miles (2km)

S M T W T F S S M T W T F S

Pub: Plough at Cadsden 01844 343302

☆ Grangelands and Pulpit Hill Nature Reserve

Plough at Cadsden

Mr Steve Hollings
Cadsden, Princes Risborough HP27 0NB
T: 01844 343302
E: info@ploughatcadsden.com
www.ploughatcadsden.com
/ 4 £95 1 £120 (£65) V Most major cards. All rooms en-suite
Evening meal on Sundays by arrangement only. Free WiFi

Askett

SP8105 1.2 miles (2km)
Monks Risborough 0.5 miles (1km)

Solis Ortu *closed 20 Dec - 20 Jan* B&B

Mrs Pamela Crockett
Aylesbury Road, Askett, Princes Risborough HP27 9LY
T: 01844 347777 **M:** 07711 600540
E: p.and.pr@btinternet.com
1 £70 1 £70 (£35) (min age 3) V Double room en-suite
Twin room has private bathroom. Internet access

Wild Rose

Great Kimble

SP8206 0.6 miles (1km)
Little Kimble 0.5 miles (1km)

S M T W T F S   S M T W T F S

Pubs: Swan 01844 275288

Swan at Great Kimble

Mr Tim Woolnough
Grove Lane, Great Kimble, Aylesbury
HP17 9TR
T: 01844 275288
E: theswangtkimble@aol.com
1 £70 2 £60 (£40) 1 £100
V DRY VISA
Most major cards. All rooms en-suite

Butlers Cross

SP8407 0.6 miles (1km)
Little Kimble 1 miles (2km)

S M T W T F S   S M T W T F S

Pub: Russell Arms 01296 622618

☆ Chiltern Brewery
T: 01296 613647
www.chilternbrewery.co.uk

Weston Turville

SP8510 1.8 miles (2.9 km)
Stoke Mandeville 1.9 miles (3km) PF

S M T W T F S   S M T W T F S

S M T W T F S   S M T W T F S

Five Bells 01296 613131 &
Chandos Arms 01296 613532
Regular bus service from Wendover

Five Bells

Mr Nathan Mitchelson
40 Main Street, Weston Turville HP22 5RW
T: 01296 613131
E: info@innkeeperslodge.com
www.innkeeperslodge.com
9 £49 2 £49 5 £49 V
VISA All major cards. All rooms en-suite
Continental breakfast. Free WiFi

Hamlet *closed 25 & 26 Dec* B&B

Mr Mark Burgess
3 Home Close, Weston Turville
HP22 5SP
T: 01296 612660 **M:** 07840 335458
E: gburg27705@talktalk.net
www.thehamletbandb.co.uk
1 £75 1 £68 (£38) 1 £33
V Some rooms ensuite

WENDOVER

SP8607 on path

Wendover

Town with full range of services, visit www.wendover-pc.gov.uk for further details. Farmers Market 3rd Sat of each month.

☆ Wendover Woods
T: 01420 520212 www.forestry.gov.uk

B&B Mayertorne Cottage

2.5 miles(4km) south of Wendover

Mr Anthony Sykes
London Road, Wendover Dean HP22 6QA
T: 01296 620830
E: anthonysykes@btconnect.com
www.mayertorne.co.uk
1 £69 1 £74 V
DRY ★★★★ One room ensuite
2 £ on application
Free WiFi. 4 days notice required for evening meal

Clematis

Red Lion

Mr Sam Hughes
High Street HP22 6DU
T: 01296 622266
E: redlionhotel.wendover@fullers.co.uk
www.fullershotels.com
16 £81 3 £81 2 £81
2 £81 V
Most major cards ★★★★ All rooms en-suite
Free WiFi

17 Icknield Close — *closed Xmas* — B&B

Mrs G Samuels
Wendover HP22 6HG
T: 01296 583285
E: grbr.samuels@ntlworld.com
2 £60 1 £30 V DRY
Free WiFi

17 Orchard Close — B&B

Mrs Thalia Lansdowne
Wendover HP22 6LN
T: 01296 623624
E: thalialansdowne@btopenworld.com
1 £40 (£35) (min age 4) V

Section 6

Wendover to Ivinghoe Beacon

This 11.8 miles (18.8km) section is the most wooded of The Ridgeway with extensive woods, many of beech, much of the way. However once the Trail reaches Pitstone Hill the final few miles are in open downland countryside reminiscent of the landscape surrounding earlier stages. As a final flourish The Ridgeway finishes on top of yet another Iron Age fort at Ivinghoe Beacon.

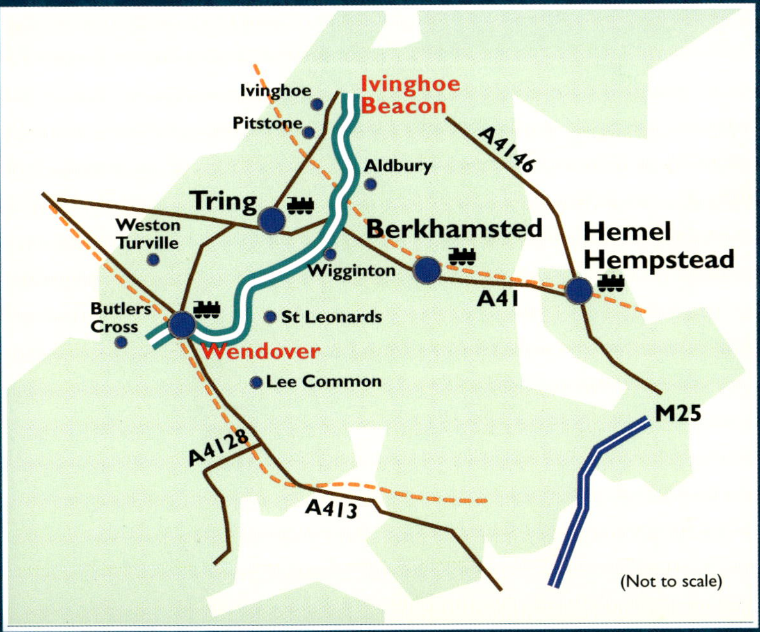

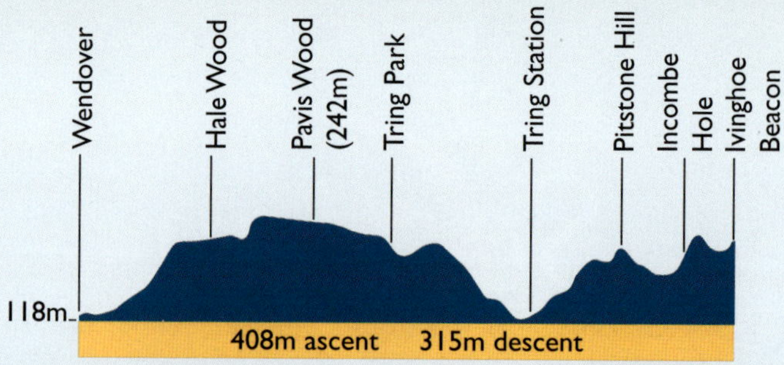

Maps

Landranger maps	165	Aylesbury and Leighton Buzzard
Explorer maps	181	Chiltern Hills North

Taxis

Place	Name	Telephone Number
Wendover	Alexander's	01296 620888
Wigginton	Diamond Cars	01442 890303
Tring	Airport Taxis of Tring	01442 828848
	Aky Cars of Tring	07958 316063
	DMG	01442 824105
	John Taxi's	01442 828828/828848
	Mike's Private Hire	01442 826161

Car Parking

If you choose to park in villages close to The Ridgeway, please park considerately. Other places to park are listed below but you need to be aware that theft from cars parked in the countryside does occur. You are advised to leave any unnecessary items at home or, failing that, ensure that anything valuable is locked in the boot of your vehicle.

Place	Map Grid Reference
Wendover public car park	SP 868077
Pitstone Hill car park east of Tring. From sharp bend on B488, ½ mile (1km) southeast of Ivinghoe, take minor road signposted Aldbury. Car park is on right after ½ mile (1km)	SP 955149
National Trust car park for Ivinghoe Beacon, on the left of minor road to Ringshall, ½ mile (1km) south off the B489	SP 962162

Toilets

Place	Map Grid Reference
Wendover (Library Car Park)	SP 868078

Vets

Place	Name	Telephone Number
Halton	Wendover Heights Veterinary Centre	01296 623439
Tring	Springwell Veterinary Surgery	01442 822151

Visitor Information Centres

These VICs are staffed but note that many libraries in the area also have leaflets about local attractions and events.

★ offers accommodation booking service (until 15:30)

Place	Address/Opening Hours
★Wendover	The Clock Tower, High Street, Wendover HP22 6DU **T**: 01296 696759 www.wendover-pc.gov.uk Opening hours: All year: Mon-Sat 10:00-16:00
Tring	99 Akeman Street, Tring HP23 6AA **T**: 01442 823347 www.tring.gov.uk Opening hours: All year: Mon-Sat 09:30-15:00, Sat 10:00-13:00

Ivinghoe Beacon from Pitstone Hill

Lee Common

SP9004 1.9 miles (3km)
Wendover 4.5 miles (7.3km)

S M T W T F S   S M T W T F S

Cock and Rabbit/Graziemille 01494 837540

B&B SC
Lower Bassibones Farm

Mrs Anthea Hartley
Lee Common, Great Missenden
HP16 9LA
T: 01494 837798
E: lowerbassibones@yahoo.co.uk
www.discover-real-england.com
2 £65 DRY Most major cards ★★★★
VisitBritain Silver Award. Self-catering accommodation also available at £295/ week

St Leonards

SP8510 2.5 miles (4 km)
Stoke Mandeville 1.9 miles (3km) PF

S M T W T F S   S M T W T F S

Pub: White Lion 01494 758387 - pub for sale as Companion went to print, so check opening times

Wigginton

SP9310 on path
Tring 1 miles (2km)

S M T W T F S   S M T W T F S

Pub: Greyhound Inn 01442 824631

☆ Tring Park
www.woodlandtrust.org.uk

Greyhound Inn - Wigginton

INN

Mr Paul Phillips
Chesham Road, Wigginton HP23 6EH
T: 01442 824631
E: the-greyhound@hotmail.co.uk
www.greyhoundtring.co.uk
1 £65 1 £65 (£50) 1 £80
V
Most major cards. All rooms en-suite
No evening meal Sundays. Free WiFi

Wendover Woods

Tring

SP9211 1.2 miles (2km)
Tring P£

Town with full range of services, visit www.tring.gov.uk for further details.

☆ The Natural History Museum Tring
T: 0207 9426171 www.nhm.ac.uk/tring

☆ Grand Union Canal
www.waterscape.com/Grand_Union_Canal

Pendley Manor Hotel

Mrs Claire Lee
Cow Lane, Tring HP23 5QY
T: 01442 891891
E: sales@pendley-manor.co.uk
www.pendley-manor.co.uk
55 £90 15 £90 2 £90 1 £90 V All major cards ★★★★ All rooms en-suite
Highly commended in Tourism Southeast's Award for Excellence. Free WiFi.

Premier Inn

The Manager
Tring Hill, Tring HP23 4LD
T: 01442 824819
E: tring.pi@premierinn.com
www.premierinn.com
30 £29 All major cards. All rooms en-suite
Prices are for room only. Restaurant serving breakfast and evening meal located on site

Rose and Crown Hotel *closed Xmas & New Year*

Mrs Claire Lee
High Street, Tring HP23 5AH
T: 01442 824071
E: salesrose.crown@pendley-manor.co.uk
www.roseandcrown-tring.co.uk
15 £59 (£49) 2 £75 4 £49 V DRY All major cards. All rooms en-suite

Aldbury

SP9612 0.6 miles (1km)
Tring 1 miles (1.5km) PF

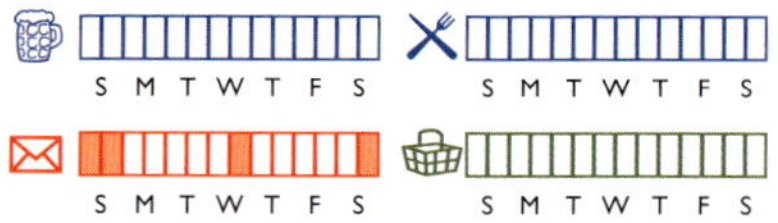

Pubs: Greyhound 01442 851228 & Valiant Trooper 01442 851203

☆ Aldbury Nowers (Duchies Piece) Nature Reserve
www.hertswildlifetrust.org.uk

☆ Ashridge Estate
T: 01494 755557
www.nationaltrust.org.uk

B&B **Folly Farm**

Mr Jude Glenister
Northfiled Road, Aldbury HP23 5QJ
T: 01442 851645
E: info@follyfarmbedandbreakfast.co.uk
www.follyfarmbedandbreakfast.co.uk
2 £75 (£70) 1 £50 V
DRY Some rooms en-suite
Private bathroom. Free WiFi. Lift to pub for evening meal

Greyhound Inn - Aldbury

Mr Tim O'Gorman
19 Stocks Road, Aldbury HP23 5RT
T: 01442 851228
E: greyhound@aldbury.wanadoo.co.uk
www.greyhoundaldbury.co.uk
8 £75 2 £75 1 £90 8 £65 V O DRY
Most major cards. All rooms en-suite

Near Aldbury Nowers

Pitstone

SP9315 1.6 miles (2.5km)
Tring 2 miles (4km) P F

S M T W T F S   S M T W T F S

S M T W T F S

In general store
Pubs: Bell (opening times unknown)

☆ Pitstone Windmill
www.nationaltrust.org.uk

☆ Pitstone Green Museum
T: 01582 851227
http://website.lineone.net/~pitstonemus

Silver Birch Campsite *closed 1 Nov - Easter*

SP947153 0.6miles(1km) from Ridgeway

Mr S Newman
Upper Icknield Way, Pitstone, Leighton Buzzard LU7 9EN
T: 01296 668348
10 £price on application

Ivinghoe

SP9416 0.9 miles (1.5km)
Tring 3 miles (5km)

S M T W T F S
S M T W T F S

S M T W T F S
S M T W T F S

In post office. Post office stocks some food
Pub: Rose & Crown 01296 668472
Café: Open November to March only

☆ Ford End Water Mill
T: 01442 825 421
www. fordendwatermill.co.uk

Brownlow

B&B

SP934175 1.2 miles (1.9km) northwest of Ivinghoe

Eric and Sue Kettler
Ivinghoe LU7 9DY
T: 01296 668787
E: info@thebrownlow.com
www.thebrownlow.com
4 £78 1 £78 (£50) (min age 10) V DRY
★★★★ All rooms en-suite
AA highly commended. Free WiFi

Town Farm

SP950164 600m east of Ivinghoe
Mrs Leach
Ivinghoe, Leighton Buzzard LU7 9EL
T: 01296 668455
E: cwleach33@yahoo.co.uk
www.townfarmcamping.co.uk
20 £10/person 10 £20 WC DRY All major cards

Near Ivinghoe Beacon

Distances between places along the The Ridgeway in miles

	Overton Hill	Ogbourne St George	Fox Hill	Uffington Castle	Sparsholt Firs	A338 (Wantage)	Bury Down	Streatley	Mongewell Park	Nuffield	Watlington	Chinnor	Princes Risborough	Wendover	Wigginton
Ogbourne St George	9.3														
Fox Hill	17.0	7.7													
Uffington Castle	22.3	13.0	5.3												
Sparsholt Firs	25.3	16.0	8.3	3.0											
A338 (Wantage)	29.1	19.8	12.1	6.8	3.8										
Bury Down	34.5	25.2	17.5	12.2	9.2	5.4									
Streatley	42.7	33.4	25.7	20.4	17.4	13.6	8.2								
Mongewell Park	48.5	39.2	31.5	26.2	23.2	19.4	14.0	5.8							
Nuffield	52.4	43.1	35.4	30.1	27.1	23.3	17.9	9.7	3.9						
Watlington	58.0	48.7	41.0	35.7	32.7	28.9	23.5	15.3	9.5	5.6					
Chinnor	63.7	54.4	46.7	41.4	38.4	34.6	29.2	21.0	15.2	11.3	5.7				
Princes Risborough	68.5	59.2	51.5	46.2	43.2	39.4	34.0	25.8	20.0	16.1	10.5	4.8			
Wendover	75.0	65.7	58.0	52.7	49.7	45.9	40.5	32.3	26.5	22.6	17.0	11.3	6.5		
Wigginton	81.5	72.2	64.5	59.2	56.2	52.4	47.0	38.8	33.0	29.1	23.5	17.8	13.0	6.5	
Ivinghoe Beacon	86.8	77.5	69.8	64.5	61.5	57.7	52.3	44.1	38.3	34.4	28.8	23.1	18.3	11.8	5.3